ANNOTATED

OPENING STATEMENTS

PET P LMA

Published by
ATLA Press
1050 31st Street, NW
Washington, DC 20007

Library of Congress Catalog Number 94-15354
ISBN 0-941916-69-3
2nd Printing

Cover design by
Marcella Kulchitsky

Table of Contents

Foreword

In 1974 when I completed law school, I entered the private practice of law, eager to become the best that I could be at the art of trial advocacy. It took me approximately 90 days to discover that although my law studies had ended after law school graduation, my study of trial skills had not even begun. Fortunately, older and more experienced colleagues of mine directed me to the Association of Trial Lawyers of America, assuring me that ATLA's educational programs would provide not only inspiration but superior instruction geared toward preparing me for simple and complex litigation. It was at my first ATLA seminar that I first encountered Peter Perlman.

We members of the trial bar will be associated with few advocates as capable as Peter Perlman. His easy style, his tremendous eloquence, and his soft touch combine to make him one of the most successful individuals in the American courtroom. In his practice, he has effectively addressed complex issues from products liability to medical negligence, always being careful to handle these issues with simplicity so that each juror understands the theory of recovery and the elements of damages. His use of analogy is legendary.

In the pages that follow, we have the opportunity to learn from Peter Perlman, an individual who has shown an uncommon willingness to share. As you sample this selection of successful opening statements, you will be able to follow his logic, his analogies, and his style. You can read forward from this page with the assurance that what is presented here will make a major contribution to your presentation of effective opening statements, whether you are an attorney beginning your study of trial advocacy or an experienced veteran seeking to fine-tune previously acquired skills.

Trial advocacy is a journey, not a destination. We are all engaged in a continuing effort to improve the way in which we present our cases to juries. Peter Perlman has emerged as a true teacher and leader of this effort. His work on opening statements is a unique treasure we can all use to improve our communication skills.

Rich Hailey
ATLA Treasurer (1993-94)

Acknowledgments

I would like to thank my daughter Pamela Perlman and my legal assistant Anne W. Miller for their patient and tireless efforts in proofing the manuscript. Also, special thanks to my assistants Cindy Taylor and Sandy Williams for their typing and research. In addition, I would like to thank my associate Bryce D. Franklin for his advice and assistance.

The support and hard work of ATLA Press staff members April Gustafson, Cathy Kruvant, Laura Rucker, and Lou Leto were essential to bringing this project to fruition. The inspiration and support of Rich Page and Jack Marshall during the inception of this ambitious project also deserve mention here.

Most of all, I want to express my appreciation to my clients, who have provided the inspiration for these cases. Late in his career, the legendary trial lawyer Clarence Darrow was charged with subornation of perjury. In his own defense, he told the jury the following:

> I have committed one crime . . . which cannot be forgiven. I have stood for the weak and the poor. I have stood for [those] who toil. . . . I have lived my life, and I have fought my battles, not against the weak and the poor—anybody can do that—but against power, against injustice, against oppression . . . .[1]

Each of the people represented in this book has stood up against power, injustice, and oppression. They have been willing to fight the battle, not only on their own behalf, but so that others would have the same right. To them I owe my deep admiration and my lifelong friendship.

---

[1] ATTORNEY FOR THE DAMNED 496, 497 (Arthur Weinberg ed., 1957).

The Opening Statement: An Overview

The psychological principle of primacy teaches us that people tend to believe the first explanation or impression they get on a topic. Accordingly, in a trial, jurors are most likely to believe the story they hear first (if they have a good impression of the storyteller). Once a first impression—whether good or bad—has been made, that impression will be readily retained and difficult to alter. Therefore, if you impress the jurors favorably with your version of the facts, your opponent will be hard pressed to change the jurors' minds.

At the beginning of the opening statement, the mood is set, the theme is expressed, and the jurors become involved in the real-life drama of the facts and circumstances of the case that is about to be discussed. To successfully involve the jurors in the case, you must consider the state of mind and the anxiety of each juror as you deliver your opening statement. The following explanation of a potential juror's attitudes will help you empathize with jurors:

> A juror's fears and concerns as he or she starts his or her job in the courtroom are very similar to yours in the doctor's office, and are based on the same set of human principles.
>
> For most jurors it's the first time they're going through this process. Someone outside their own lives has asked them to make a momentous and consequential decision: A binding judgment that will affect someone else's life, a judgment of who's right and wrong and how to mete out punishment. Picture their anxiety. Housed in an unfamiliar setting, they are being asked to perform, to deal with and to handle a major procedure for the

> first time without knowing what's to come or if they can do it as well as they'd like to. What could help them relax and get to work, to quell those anxious inner voices and focus on you and the trial?[2]

To address the needs of the jury and to present the case in its most favorable light, you should try to do the following:

- Orient the jurors by giving them adequate background for your story.
- Persuade the jurors by commanding their attention.[3]
- Project your sincerity and your belief in the rightness of your cause.
- Involve the jurors through an effective storytelling method and through helping them identify with your client.
- Elicit the jurors' sympathy as you develop and present the human aspects of the case.

If your attempts are sincere and well organized and if your case is solid, you will make a good first impression. An excellent book written by an able trial lawyer, Alfred Julien, on the subject of opening statements describes the importance of the first impression.

> The first impression is most important. In jurisdictions where counsel may personally interrogate the jury, the preliminary impressions have already begun. But in the opening, the narrative, the outline of the flesh and bones of the case, the jury's first impressions harden like cement. *No amount of instruction from the court that minds should not be made up until the conclusion of the case can prevent people from forming impressions.* Impressions of counsel, impressions of the honesty of his outline, impressions of the bona

---

2 SONYA HAMLIN, WHAT MAKES JURIES LISTEN 105–06 (1985).

3 *See* Russ M. Herman, *The Opening Statement: Using It to Maximum Advantage,* TRIAL, Aug. 1989, at 72.

fides of his case, all can combine to win a case in opening. This is the psychological effect of primacy. *(Emphasis added.)*[4]

The late, well-known author and humorist Lewis Grizzard identified the concept of primacy from his perspective as an author:

> My theory is that if somebody goes into a bookstore and starts browsing through a book, whether or not they buy it probably depends on how they enjoy the first few pages. You can't stand around in a bookstore and read an entire book and then put it back on the shelf, thereby actually *stealing* the book, unless, of course, it is *very* short, which is why most writers make their books so long. Tolstoy, for instance, was so concerned about somebody doing that to *War and Peace* that he wrote one of the longest books in the history of books.
>
> So I'm going for the sensational and the prurient early, figuring the browser might say, "Hey, this is pretty exciting stuff. I'd better buy this book so I don't miss what else is in it."[5]

Similarly, if the first few paragraphs of your opening statement hook your listeners—the jurors—they'll probably "buy" your story.

The Beginning of Your Opening Statement—Be Creative

In many cases, the first two minutes of the opening statement are the most critical minutes of the entire trial. During this time, you should always take advantage of primacy and pave the way for persuading the jury to believe your side of the story.

Consider the following:

> He was a Boy Scout, a Little Leaguer, and a varsity football player who worked hard to get B's in high school. He loved John Wayne movies. He was popular at school and was adored at home. His mother thought he was the most handsome boy in Ashland, Kentucky.

---

4 ALFRED S. JULIEN, OPENING STATEMENTS § 1.01 (1991).

5 LEWIS GRIZZARD, IF I EVER GET BACK TO GEORGIA, I'M GONNA NAIL MY FEET TO THE GROUND 8 (1990).

Although this is not an opening statement but the beginning of a newspaper tribute to a soldier who was killed in the Vietnam War, it contains elements essential to an opening statement like developing human aspects of the case that will help the jury identify with your client. Most importantly, it captures its audience's interest.

Command the Jury's Attention

Effective persuasion requires that the opening statement command the jury's attention. One way to get that attention is to use a simple newspaper style of storytelling. Consider the following news story:

> A 12-year-old boy who dreamed of becoming a marine biologist died after he was hit by a school bus that drove onto the sidewalk in front of his grade school. *Cincinnati Enquirer*, Mar. 30, 1990.

This paragraph is brief yet thorough, and it immediately focuses the audience's attention on a victim.

An excellent opening statement that immediately put an entire case into focus was given by Tom Riley in a case involving toxic shock syndrome. The case was brought in Cedar Rapids, Iowa, against Procter & Gamble on the theory that the manufacturer produced a defective product and withheld vital information from the public, particularly from the women who used the product. The first words the attorney said to the jury during the opening statement were like a news story, with the bare action and tragedy of the story right there in the first two sentences:

> On September 2, 1980, Michael Kehm's wife, Pat, used Rely tampons for the first time. Four days later she was dead.[6]

The *Los Angeles Times'* coverage of an airplane crash involving a Wings West airplane included the following paragraphs:

---

6 The summary of this litigation is contained in Tom Riley's book, THE PRICE OF LIFE 154 (1986).

> Derek Davies had just learned how to rope horses, and he was on his way to break in his new skills on an uncle's ranch in Nevada—one of the grandest adventures that a 13-year-old boy from this scenic California city could imagine.
>
> Linda Da Silva, 18, had interrupted her freshman year at Cuesta Community College here [in San Luis Obispo] and plans for her debutante ball in Newport Beach so that she could attend her brother's wedding in Seattle.
>
> These were the special dreams of two ordinary teen-agers—dreams that ended in a few nightmarish moments when a small Wings West airliner collided in the air Friday with a private airplane above a hilly area just inside the city limits.[7]

Involve the Jury

The jury needs to become involved in the case from the outset. A storytelling method that uses analogies and imagery is the most effective way to get jurors involved. Additionally, you should be sure to use every opportunity you have to help the jurors identify with your client.

Consider the following reference from the book *What Makes Juries Listen*:

> There is much in any trial that is instantly identifiable, images that can be brought to everyone's mind. Yet unfortunately, lawyers often lose sight of the fact that a case is a narrative, that stories have appealed to all peoples from the beginning of time. In wanting to get out the facts and a listing of the issues, you can forget that people don't like listening to dry data to which they don't relate and which reminds them of those abstract math problems at school.
>
> A story has built-in charisma. Little children say, "Tell me a story." Someone who calls you on the phone saying, "Have I got a story to tell you," makes you eagerly lean forward and listen. You listen because you anticipate elements of pleasure or surprise, the ability to use your own fantasy and imagination to enter into it, and a chance to remove yourself from your own life and live someone else's for a little while.

---

7 Patricia Klein & Mark Stein, *Dreams of 2 Young Lives Consumed in Fiery Crash*, L.A. TIMES, Aug. 26, 1984, at I3.

> Why are soap operas so incredibly successful in this country? It's because people feel, "There's enough in it that looks like my life. Yet other things happen that never happened to me. I'd love to extend myself into someone else's experiences for a while, with no risk." That's a basic, compelling drive that is always and forever interesting to any audience, that will make them listen.
>
> Begin with a tease, a glimpse into where you're going and a little excitement about what's going to happen next. Use the story in your trial to begin your narrative. Instead of saying, "Ladies and gentlemen, this case deals with certain issues of compensation which the law provides . . . ," begin with "The story begins on a Sunday morning;" or "Imagine looking out the window and watching the rain." Or "On a day just like this, snowing and blustery, Marion Snodgrass got in her car and was driving down Maple Street right here in town."[8]

A masterful treatise entitled *Art of Advocacy: Opening Statement* also discusses the importance of telling an effective story.[9]

> Opening statement is simply story telling. If you can present your case to the jurors in a clean, simple, understandable way, maintaining their interest and accomplishing the various objectives we shall talk about, you have done your job.

Simplify, Simplify

Simplicity must be one of your major objectives. It is the trial lawyer's responsibility to reduce complicated facts or technical matters to simple, common explanations that can be easily understood by an average jury. Above all, you must avoid legalistic jargon or "lawyer talk."

Winston Churchill said it well: "Short words are best and the old words when short are best of all." In other words, besides choosing words with fewer syllables, you should use words that are well established in the language; avoid trendy words and jargon.

---

8 HAMLIN, *supra* note 2, at 119.

9 LEONARD DECOF, ART OF ADVOCACY: OPENING STATEMENT § 1.04, AT 1–10 (1982 & SUPP. 1991).

Certain words and phrases naturally bring images of force, impact, and action to listeners' minds. Using these words and phrases—like *collided, mangled, impaled, crushed, cooked,* and *buried alive*—can make themes and descriptions stronger.

Carefully chosen expressions you use during the opening statement frequently form themes for the entire case. For example, a quadriplegic is "a prisoner in his own body," and a child who has suffered burn injuries is described in the opening statement thus: "She will never be a stranger to the burn unit of the children's hospital."

Simple descriptions are more effective than tedious and technical ones. For example, most tragedies occur instantaneously, but "instantaneously" is not the word to use. No matter how hard you try, you can't say it any better than "It happened as quick as the snap of a finger."

Adages and proverbs can be effective in promoting the jurors' identification with your client and case. Some good ones to use are the following:

- A chain is only as strong as its weakest link.
- A small hole can sink a big ship.
- Actions speak louder than words.
- Birds of a feather flock together.
- Familiarity breeds contempt.
- The fruit never falls far from the tree.
- There is no such thing as a nonworking mother.

Be careful not to put up roadblocks to the jury's understanding. One roadblock that distracts the jury from concentrating on the facts at hand is the use of redundant or meaningless words and phrases. Consider the following examples:

- close proximity,
- exact same,
- 24 hours a day,

- new innovation,
- minor emergency,
- all except, and
- preplanning.

Rather than using repetitive phrases, you should use clear, straightforward speech that gets your point across in as few words and syllables as possible.

Discussing the Amount

Even among outstanding trial lawyers, there is much controversy over the question of whether to discuss dollar amounts in the opening statement. In some jurisdictions, the choice is made for you because lawyers are not permitted to discuss the amount of the prayer either during jury selection or opening statement.

It's my opinion that when you do have the choice, sometimes you should discuss the dollar amount sought and sometimes you shouldn't. If the case has merit and the damages are significant and supportable, you shouldn't have any hesitation about discussing amounts in the opening statement. When you discuss amounts, you will predispose the jury to think about the case in substantial terms. In fact, a failure to mention damages in the opening statement may suggest that you lack faith in the merits of your case.

The topic of damages is of common interest to laypeople, the media, and even other lawyers who will probably ask how much you sued for, but the decision of whether to discuss amounts during opening statement is a strategic one that must be made by individual counsel based on the circumstances of each case. In many instances, mentioning dollars in the opening may be a dangerous and questionable tactic.[10]

---

[10] FREDRIC G. LEVIN, EFFECTIVE OPENING STATEMENTS: THE ATTORNEY'S MASTER KEY TO COURTROOM VICTORY (1983). *See also* BERTRAM G. WARSHAW, TRIAL MASTERS: A HANDBOOK OF STRATEGIES & TECHNIQUES THAT WIN CASES (1984).

Some lawyers attempt to walk the line between mentioning money and not mentioning it. These lawyers will use the opening statement to extensively detail the liability aspects of their case and then, at the end of the opening statement, they will give dollar amounts for the "special damages" like medical bills and follow by asking the jury to make an award that is fair and reasonable.

This approach, which parallels the insurance industry's time-honored practice of evaluating cases on the basis of the special damages, should be rejected by competent trial lawyers because it simply does not stand up to a commonsense analysis. When a person has been injured and hospitalized, would a friend, relative, or neighbor be expected to ask, "How much were the medical expenses?" No; this would be absurd. The natural response to the situation would be to inquire about the severity of the person's injury and the extent to which previous activities have been limited. These—not the amounts of hospital bills—are the true measures of suffering.

For this reason, you should spell out in your opening statement the different elements of damages and the effect your client's injuries have had on his or her routine activities.

Be Careful, Be Consistent, Be Clear

I've learned many things over my years of practice about how to give effective opening statements. The following are some guidelines I think are particularly helpful:

- Always begin with "May it please the court." It is important to always show respect for the court.
- Keep your promises. Never say you will prove something unless you are absolutely sure you can prove it. If certain evidence might be excluded or subject to a court ruling, don't make a promise regarding that evidence.
- Expose unavoidable weaknesses in your case and explain how they have little, if any, effect on the main issues of liability and damages.

- Emphasize any flaws in your opponent's case.[11]
- Explain the nature of expert testimony.
- Explain any technical terms that will be heard during the trial.
- Use demonstrative evidence. Remember that a picture is worth a thousand words.
- Explain the legal procedures that will be involved in the case—explain to the jurors the trial process and what will be expected of them as jurors.
- Ask for "the rule." "The rule," as it is commonly called by trial lawyers, prohibits witnesses who are going to testify from listening to other testimony given in the case.
- Be positive and avoid disclaimers.
- Speak in plain English and avoid legal references.
- The following outline may be helpful:

    Headline (including human terms and damages)

    Introduction and identification

    Orientation

    Description

    Injuries

    Damages

    Conclusion

- Avoid improper use of opening statement. Generally, any statement that would be considered improper in summation would also be considered improper in opening statement. The following are definitely improper:

---

[11] ROBERT JOSSEN, MASTER ADVOCATES HANDBOOK 65 (National Inst. of Trial Advocacy, 1986).

- addressing a juror by name,
- referring to the results of another case,
- referring to evidence excluded by pretrial rulings,
- referring to matters outside the evidence,
- referring to hearsay evidence that may not be admitted,
- referring to a former trial of the same case,
- referring to liability insurance,
- using medical or learned treatises,
- reading from a law book or statute,
- appealing to any juror's self-interest,
- appealing to the financial status of the parties,
- attacking opposing counsel,
- asking jurors to place themselves in the shoes of the litigants (the Golden Rule),
- making any statement whose purpose is primarily to appeal to sympathy or to incite passion or prejudice, and
- using argument.[12]

Concluding Your Opening Statement

At the conclusion of your opening statement, you should return to your damages theme and end on a high note. For example, in *Sexton v. Bell Helmets*, the helmet case printed in this book, the opening statement concludes like this:

---

[12] RICHARD H. UNDERWOOD & WILLIAM H. FORTUNE, TRIAL ETHICS § 10.5 (1988 & Supp. 1990).

> Earlier we talked about the catastrophic damages that were caused by this dangerous product and the closed-head injury which Chad must live with for the rest of his life. The evidence will be that the cost of therapy treatments and rehabilitation will exceed two million dollars. We know that is a large amount of money, and when you have heard the evidence in this case, you will learn that this is a most reasonable amount and totally justified by the evidence and circumstances involved. Chad has a 54-year life expectancy, and your decision in this case will have to stand for all time.

In the examples of opening statements presented in this book, you'll notice that I use the word "we" whenever possible. I think this identification technique is one that you must use to involve the jurors and show them that you are concerned with meeting your client's needs rather than your own.[13] You must show the jurors that you, the attorney, are really just a person with human emotions, trying to help your client.

Finally, your words and actions during opening statement must build a strong and believable foundation for your case. The renowned British barrister Sir Edward Marshall Hall said,

> A lawyer and an actor are akin. It is true I have no mask, I have no set lines, I have no black cloth and I have no floodlights to help bring illusion; but out of the miseries and the joys and the strivings and experience of men, I must create an atmosphere of living reality so that it may be felt and understood by others, for that is advocacy.

Creating this "atmosphere of living reality" should be a main objective of your opening statement.

* * *

There are several reasons that this edition of *Opening Statements* has been annotated. First, I felt that the first edition was simply a collection of transcripts that lacked useful background information about the various cases, so this edition provides case summaries before each opening statement. Second, I thought it would be helpful

---

13 DECOF, *supra* note 9, § 1.08[4].

for my audience, trial lawyers, to see analyses of the thought processes that went into the various opening statements. Thus I have supplied analytical annotations of the opening statements themselves. Third, I wanted to obtain some input from some of the nation's best trial lawyers to provide different, more objective perspectives, so I annotated only four of the opening statements in this book and recruited guest annotators to analyze the other five.

The trial lawyers I asked to annotate opening statements gave unselfishly of their time and vast experience to lend some of their insights and observations. All the annotators I chose are outstanding trial lawyers, and I am indebted to them for their significant contributions to this book.

Chapter 1

Moore v. New Idea Farm Equipment Company

Although the *Moore v. New Idea Farm Equipment Co.*[14] trial was held more than a decade ago and the Model 7 corn picker involved in the case was designed over 50 years ago, Darrell Moore's injury is typical of farm injuries today. The bitter toll that is still being exacted in farm machinery tragedies demonstrates how little progress has been made in the design of farm equipment over the years. According to the National Safety Council, farming is the most hazardous job in America,[15] and a study by the Texas Department of Agriculture shows that the safety records of farm machinery are actually worsening.[16] The Texas study found that between 1930 and 1980 the number of deaths in the United States caused by farm machines increased by 44 percent while the rate of deaths caused by all other machinery decreased by 80 percent. In 1987, 49 out of every 100,000 farmers in

---

[14] Moore v. New Idea Farm Equip. Co., No. 78-CI069 (Lee County Cir. Ct., Beattyville, Ky. May 1, 1981).

[15] NATIONAL SAFETY COUNCIL, SAFETY AND HEALTH: NATIONAL SAFETY COUNCIL PRELIMINARY ESTIMATES FOR 1987 (May 1988).

[16] TEXAS DEP'T OF AGRIC., REGULATORY DIV., AGRICULTURE AND TORT REFORM (1987). This subject is addressed in the study, THE BITTER HARVEST: FARM SAFETY IN AMERICA, available from the Civil Justice Foundation, 1050 31st Street N.W., Washington, D.C. 20007.

the United States died in farm-machine-related accidents—that rate is five times the national average for all major industries.

Moore v. New Idea Farm Equipment Co. was a typical farm injury case. On the day he was injured, Darrell Moore, a 24-year-old farm worker, was helping Herbert Noe, an experienced farmer, harvest corn using a corn picker pulled behind a tractor driven by Mr. Noe. Often during that day, the husking rollers located in the rear of the corn picker became clogged with corn, husks, and debris. Darrell sat on the sideboard of the tractor, and when the corn picker clogged, he got off the tractor and went back to clean out the husking rollers. As I explain in more detail in the opening statement, Mr. Noe did not disengage the tractor or disconnect the power takeoff unit while Darrell cleaned the rollers. These issues were stressed extensively by the manufacturer in this case because under the state's prevailing law at the time, any contributory negligence was a total bar on recovery.

While Darrell was trying to pull a stalk out of the roller, his left hand was sucked up into the rollers, and several of his fingers were severed. Darrell's educational background and communication skills were limited, and the impairment to his left hand caused by these injuries severely restricted his ability to perform manual labor.

The case was tried in an agricultural community. Before the trial, we did a community survey and found that the people most critical of farmers were other farmers. We also found from the survey that most farmers felt that they may have done the same thing Darrell did in trying to unclog the machine, but they knew what a serious risk the corn picker poses. They felt that someone like Darrell was at least partially responsible for his own injuries.

Part of our trial strategy was to compare the knowledge of the manufacturer with that of an uneducated farm laborer. While the farm laborer may recognize in a general way that the power takeoff should be shut off when he dismounts the tractor, he does not fully appreciate the risk of injury or the magnitude of the risk posed by leaving the power takeoff on. In contrast, the manufacturer has known for many years about the severity of the risk and the severity of the consequences.

Our theory was that the corn picker was defective and unreasonably dangerous for the following reasons:

- It was foreseeable that the corn picker's husking rollers would need to be unclogged.
- It was also foreseeable that farm workers would leave the power takeoff connected while unclogging the rollers as this provided some power for the unclogging operation.
- The manufacturer had failed to provide mechanical means to unclog the machine, even though such means were known and available when the machine was designed in 1949.
- The manufacturer had failed to warn farm workers of any hazards associated with the use or misuse of the machine.
- The manufacturer had failed to incorporate an emergency stopping device as part of the machine design.
- The manufacturer had failed to incorporate a mechanical means of either unclogging or reversing the rollers once they become clogged.

In my opening statement, I chose to personalize Darrell Moore and to describe his injuries before discussing how he was injured. Then I stated the theme in the following manner:

> This corn picker was made in 1949, so at the time of these injuries it was almost 30 years old. Yet you will learn that it was dangerous at the time it was made. It was dangerous based on basic design and engineering principles at that time. It had no control in the back where you could start and stop the rollers; there were no guards; there were no shields; and there was no effective way to unclog the machine.

The case resulted in a favorable verdict: the jury found that Darrell Moore was not responsible to any degree for his injuries and awarded him a substantial sum.

Opening Statement

May it please the court, distinguished counsel for the various parties in this case, and ladies and gentlemen of the jury. You have already heard some of the facts about this case, and you've learned that it's a case involving injuries that Darrell Moore suffered when his left hand got trapped in a corn picker. Darrell was 24 years old—according to the evidence in this case, and that is what the attorneys have to talk to you about during this part of the case, the opening statement, what the evidence in the case will be—24 years old in November of 1977, a lifelong resident of Lee County, with three brothers and three sisters, and he had done some farm work, some carpentry work, and for about two weeks before the date he was hurt he had been working as a night watchman for a coal company that is no longer here.

* * *

> **COMMENT:** Although in the opening paragraph I primarily discuss Darrell, I also briefly state the theme of the case: Darrell suffered injuries "when his left hand got trapped in a corn picker." I choose the word "trapped" for its graphic impact and use it constantly throughout the trial.
>
> We are fortunate in the manufacturer's choice of experts: one of the defense experts, who is an elderly gentleman by the time of this trial, wrote an article in 1947 in which he criticized corn pickers because "These machines have an inherent danger in them; they take people's hands." This makes for an effective line of cross-examination and sets up our theme for summation. It also ties in well with the description I give in the beginning of the opening statement of how Darrell's hand was trapped in the corn picker.

* * *

Darrell has had some speech problems from birth. He was born with a cleft palate. The proof will be that he worked nonetheless, went to school, and graduated from Lee County High School, and that it didn't affect his ability to work or to use his hands. The evidence will be that today as he sits here he suffers a major disability. He has totally lost the index finger and the middle finger and part of the ring finger on his left hand. There is only one doctor who has testified in this case, and you will hear his testimony by deposition. That doctor, Dr. Coats, is a plastic surgeon in Lexington, and he will testify that Darrell has more than a half of impairment to his whole left hand, 49 percent to his entire left arm, and 29 percent to his entire body by reason of these injuries.

Darrell had two hospitalizations—one a longer one, and one for two or three days—four operations, and various forms of surgery—wires in his hand, skin graft—and for three weeks he had to wear his left hand attached to his right shoulder.

* * *

COMMENT: At first glance, Darrell's injuries may not seem extremely serious. However, Darrell was born with a communication disorder and had only been able to perform manual labor. For this reason, we assert that he has suffered a "major disability." Damages are a difficult hurdle for us in this case because Darrell earned only $300 per month for the 10-month period before he was injured. To compensate for this fact, we argue that the measure of damages is the destruction of the power to earn money, not the destruction of income from a particular job or occupation. Despite Darrell's minimal earning history, the jury verdict in this case includes a substantial award for impairment of earning capacity.

* * *

We'll learn what caused these injuries, and we'll learn that Darrell was working for Herbert Noe, helping him pick some corn on November 11, 1977, when he had his left hand up pulling some husks down out of a corn picker. The rollers started rolling when he had his hand on a corn husk, and the corn picker took the husk up into the rollers and took his hand up in there with it, and his hand became trapped by the corn picker.

We'll learn in this case about the corn picker: how it's made, how it's designed, its age, and a lot of things of that nature. Darrell Moore had had little experience with corn pickers—he had been around them maybe five or six times—and it is significant that this is the only time he ever cleaned one out in the field. The evidence will be that Mr. Noe called for Darrell at Darrell's home and picked him up and took him out to a farm owned by Mr. Hieronymus to pick corn for a gentleman named Donnie Coomer. Now, some of these names may mean something to you, but they're not really parties in this case. They are just kind of on the fringe of the case.

* * *

COMMENT: The key language in this sequence is the description of the machine taking the corn husk up into the rollers, as well as "the corn picker took the husk up into the rollers and took his hand up in there with it, and his hand became trapped by the corn picker." Our theme in this case is that, based on what the average farm worker knew, Darrell exercised ordinary care. If he had had the same knowledge as the engineers who designed the machine, he may have done something different. This theme is presented in the closing argument in the following manner:

> I'm sure you remember the quotation from President Lincoln, who said, "God must have loved the common man, because he made so many of them." This machine was made for the common man; it wasn't made for the engineer. It may be easy for these engineers to say, "Hey, Darrell, we know how dangerous that machine is; we know how fast those rollers move; we know it will take a two-foot stalk of corn and your hand with it in two-tenths of a second, and we know that when you're in there trying to clean that machine out and you've got your hand in that opening, you can't see up above that opening, and you don't know where those rollers are working up there three inches above the opening; we know that, but you don't."

We introduce testimony from the landowner that he had cleaned the corn picker out with the power running every time it got clogged. We also introduce the testimony of several other farmers who did the same thing. A local salesman for a farm implement company testifies that he always cleaned out a corn picker with the power running. I ask him how many times he did that and he responds "I can't even think of the number of times I've done that."

To this day, it is common practice for farmers to clean out clogged corn pickers manually. The machines are designed in such a way that the farmer has few alternatives, and I know that I need to stress this to the jury from the beginning.

* * *

Let me show you some pictures of that corn picker. [See Exhibits 1, 2, 3, and 4 on pages 22–24.] That's the side view; we will introduce that picture later and let you all look at it close at hand. When the corn picker is used out in the field, it's attached from the front to a tractor, with a wagon behind it; that's the side view of the corn picker. That's a back view of the corn picker, and that's the part where Darrell was when his hand got trapped up in the husking rollers, and this picture shows that back part a little bit closer. And you can see that opening in there; that's where the husks were caught. These pictures show this enclosure here—the husking rollers are up in here—and that opening, that's where Darrell's hand was when he was pulling the husking rolls down. You will hear more about the corn picker, and you will see those pictures and a lot of exhibits in this case.

* * *

COMMENT: In this sequence, I want to present the dilemma faced by a farmer or farm worker when the corn picker becomes clogged. To unclog the rollers, he must reach into an area that is hidden from view. It is certainly foreseeable that the worker will manually pull on the corn husks, and that's precisely the reason an opening is designed in the machine beneath the husking rollers.

Exhibit 1: Rear view of corn picker.

Exhibit 2: Front view of corn picker.

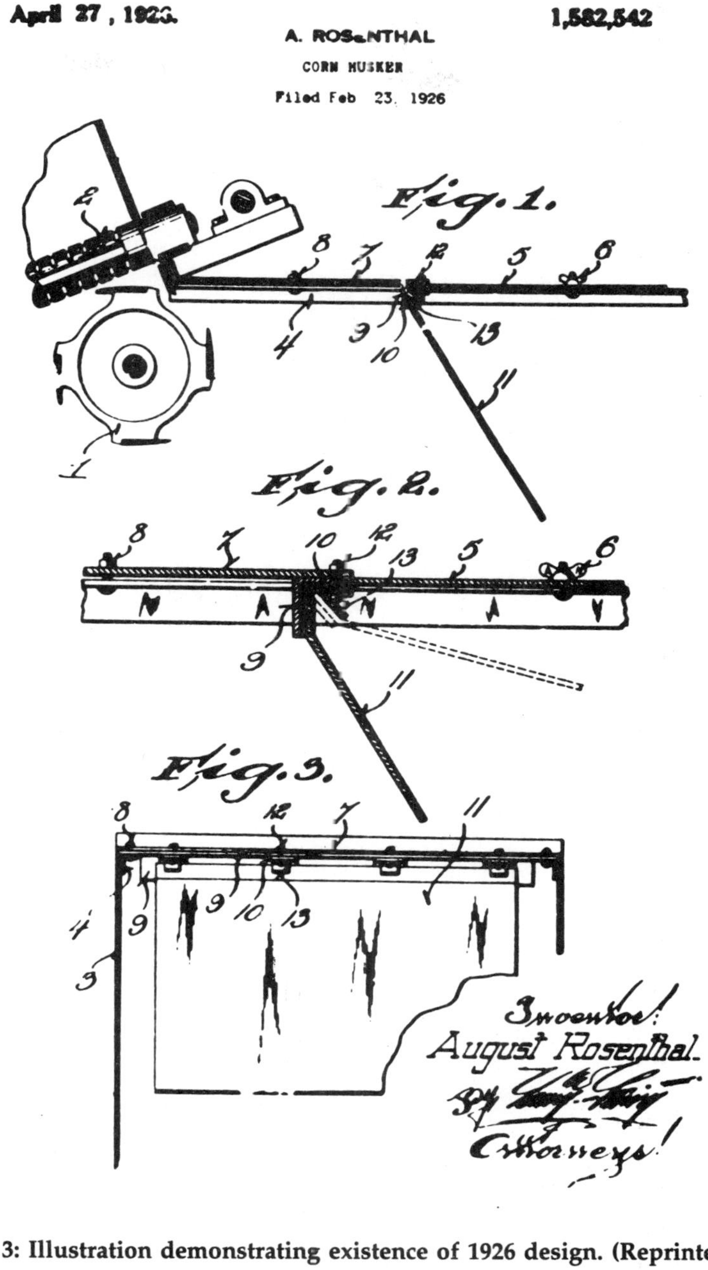

Exhibit 3: Illustration demonstrating existence of 1926 design. (Reprinted from the book, *Machine Guarding: A Historical Perspective,* courtesy of Verne L. Roberts and the Institute of Product Safety.)

Jan. 2, 1940. H. L. ROSENTHAL ET AL 2,185,739

CORN HUSKER AND SHREDDER

Filed Oct. 31, 1938

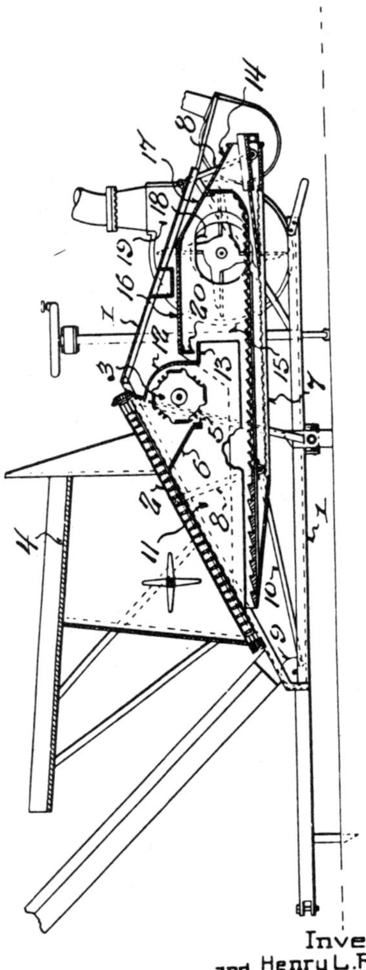

Inventors
and Henry L. Rosenthal
August Rosenthal

By [signature]

Attorneys.

Exhibit 4: Illustration demonstrating existence of 1940 protective design.

When the corn picker got clogged, Mr. Noe, who was operating the tractor, said, "Darrell, I'm going to clean out the front part; you go back and clean out the back part." Darrell had worked with Mr. Noe before, he had known him, he had been friends with him and socialized with him and had dinner at his home, and he took orders from Mr. Noe when Mr. Noe gave him orders. Mr. Noe gave Darrell orders to clean out the back of the corn picker, Darrell said, "How do you want me to do it?", and Mr. Noe said, "Use your hands." Mr. Noe was an experienced farmer and when the rollers became clogged, he did not disengage the power takeoff. The power takeoff is what connects the corn picker to the tractor, and there is a clutch on the tractor that disengages the corn picker; this was not disengaged by Mr. Noe. If there was any danger there in doing that, Mr. Noe didn't tell Darrell about it.

* * *

> **COMMENT:** In this section, I contrast the difference in knowledge and experience between Mr. Noe and Darrell. Mr. Noe had a great deal of experience, and he gave Darrell directions to follow. Darrell simply followed the directions of his employer. I want to plant the thought that if there was any negligence in the failure to disconnect the power before unclogging the rollers, Mr. Noe should be held accountable rather than Darrell.
>
> I carry this thought over into the closing argument in the following manner:
>
>> When you need a job, you do what you're asked. When you need to rely on a friend, you do what he asks you to do; you follow directions. Darrell Moore needed both.

* * *

You will hear from the evidence that the way that the corn picker was cleaned out was common practice, and people did it that way. The way the corn picker is designed, when it clogs you generally leave the equipment running because otherwise you can't see where it's clogged; this is not only the way that Darrell did it but the way others have done it.

COMMENT: The engineering testimony we present in the trial explains why farmers typically clean out the rollers with the power running: when the power is disconnected, the gathering chains and feed rollers furnish no assistance in loosening and moving the stalks. When the power is disconnected, the worker must use manual force to unclog the rollers. This takes much greater effort and, more importantly, much more time than unclogging the machine with the power on. Since the equipment clogs under power, it should have a built-in means of unclogging under power.[17]

* * *

This corn picker was made in 1949, so at the time of these injuries it was almost 30 years old. Yet you will learn that it was dangerous at the time it was made. It was dangerous based on basic design and engineering principles at that time. It had no control in the back where you could start and stop the rollers; there were no guards; there were no shields; and there was no effective way to unclog the machine.

* * *

COMMENT: One of the main defenses in the case is that the manufacturers are not responsible for Darrell's injuries because the corn picker was 30 years old. To counter that defense, I make it clear from the beginning that the safety devices that should have been incorporated into the basic design of this machine were known, available, and feasible when the machine was made in 1949. We introduce evidence later in the trial that the safety features and technology were known and available as far back as 1926. We introduce patents that were issued in 1926 and 1940 for the protection of a worker's hand while the worker unclogs the husking rollers.

---

[17] Parks v. Allis-Chalmers Corp., 289 N.W.2d 456 (Minn. 1979) contains an excellent legal opinion that discusses such a design.

The evidence will be that there was one sign on this machine, and it was a great big machine. The only kind of sign was a small decal three inches by four inches—that's about the size of a business card—and it was on the side of the machine. This sign cautioned about moving parts, but the evidence will show that the sign was not where the danger was. If you look at the entire back of the machine, where those moving rollers are, you can see that there's not one sign on that back part, not one sign.

* * *

COMMENT: Another major defense in this case is the manufacturer's claim that it furnished, but the farmer violated, a warning that provided the following:

- Disengage power takeoff while unclogging the corn picker.

- Keep hands, feet, and clothing away from power-driven parts.

It is our position that the warnings are totally inadequate. We present expert testimony along the following lines:

- In safety engineering, a warning is never enough if the hazard can be reasonably eliminated.

- A warning is never enough if the risk of harm can be reasonably eliminated.

- An effective warning must warn the user of all hazards and risks, not simply provide a disclaimer for the manufacturer.[18]

In addition, under Kentucky law, "adequate warning" is defined as the degree of warning that gives the user of the equipment "fair and adequate notice of the possible

---

[18] *See* Harry M. Philo, *New Dimensions in the Tortious Failure to Warn*, TRIAL, Nov. 1981, at 40, 42.

consequences of use or even misuse" of the equipment.[19]

It is our position that the manufacturer, New Idea Corporation, failed to provide adequate warning within the meaning of the law and that even if there was some misuse of the equipment, the misuse should not be a bar to our recovery.

* * *

Darrell relied on the superior knowledge of the man he was working for and on the people who made the machine. He will tell you that when his hand got caught up in there, it was just like that—there was no time to react, there was no time to do anything about it—his hand got caught, and he was a prisoner of the machine. This will be the evidence.

* * *

COMMENT: Our expert evidence later demonstrates that the unreasonably dangerous design of the corn picker both included and hid from Darrell the hazard of the husking rollers. Our expert testifies that the rollers turn at approximately 550 revolutions per minute. Our position is that the hazard is not caused by a person's placing a hand in the opening, but rather by a person's grabbing a clogged corn husk and not being able to let go in time after the picker is unclogged and the rollers become active. The expert's description includes the following testimony:

> If a farmer took hold of a stalk two feet long, it would take two-tenths of a second from the time the end of the stalk was caught in the roll until his hand was caught. The reaction time for an active, athletic adult male is about four- to five-tenths of a second.

In other words, the manufacturer knew when the machine was designed that an operator's hand that was on a corn stalk clogging the machine could be jerked into the rollers before the operator could release the stalk. The

[19] Post v. American Cleaning Equip. Corp., 437 S.W.2d 516, 520 (Ky. 1968).

manufacturer also knew that a person caught with one arm up in the rollers would be a helpless victim and a "prisoner of the machine."

* * *

You will hear from several engineers who will testify that basic design engineering principles require a company that makes this kind of machine to do several things in designing the machine. They include number one, identifying the hazard; number two, eliminating the hazard. The proof will be in this case that it was not eliminated. Number three, that if they can't eliminate the hazard, to guard against it. The proof will be that they didn't do that. Number four, if they can't eliminate the hazard and if they can't guard against the hazard, then to give a fair and adequate warning. The proof will be in this case that they didn't do that.

* * *

COMMENT: In this portion of the opening statement, I advise the jury that certain basic engineering principles were violated. This "preview of coming attractions" summarizes the expert engineering testimony that I will present later in our case. These basic engineering principles should apply to almost every case involving a defective product.[20]

This theme is also addressed in the closing argument in the following manner:

> Many years ago it was the practice—and manufacturers of these implements believe it's still the practice—to say, "Let the buyer beware; be careful, user, be careful." Think about that philosophy. And they still say that that should be the policy. Think about that philosophy. What they're saying is, "You be careful, and that ends our responsibility to design a

---

[20] *See* an analysis of hazard and risk recognition at HARRY M. PHILO, LAWYERS DESK REFERENCE ch. 22 (7th ed. 1987 & Supp. 1992). *See also* the discussion of this subject in SCOTT BALDWIN ET AL., THE PREPARATION OF A PRODUCT LIABILITY CASE § 1.3 (2d ed. 1993).

safe product." If they built the product safely to begin with and designed the hazards out of it, there wouldn't be any issue about being careful. They still operate that way, and they tell you that since 1929 there have been no major safety design changes in that entire corn picker. This philosophy is not what the law says in these instructions. The judge in these instructions doesn't tell you that that's the law in Lee County, Kentucky; and the reason is because the maker, the seller, and the designer of a product create a risk. They reap the benefits, and they should stand behind a product when somebody gets hurt. One of these instructions talks about the risk versus the benefit. What's the risk—5 percent, 6 percent—and they were arguing, "Well, 434 out of 70,000; how much is that?" It's 6.2 percent. Is that an acceptable risk—or is one too many? For Darrell Moore and James Christian and the others, one is too many, and if the manufacturers can design the product safely to begin with, there is no risk that is acceptable. If it's an acceptable risk, let *them* accept it. They designed the product and hundreds of thousands of others just like it.

* * *

Darrell relied on Mr. Noe and on the experience and design safety engineering of the company. He was furnished by both with an unsafe piece of equipment to work on. For the last three and a half years he has had to assume the burden of these injuries. The question that the jury will be presented with at the end of the case will be what's the value for a man to go through life without the full use of his two hands.

Chapter 2

Riffe v. International Harvester

Don Riffe, a 38-year-old coal mine equipment operator, worked for Wolfe Creek Collieries in Martin County, Kentucky. He was killed on February 8, 1978, when an International Harvester Hough H-65-C front-end loader rolled over and crushed him. *Riffe v. International Harvester*[21] was a products liability suit brought against the end loader's manufacturer by Lou Raines Riffe, Mr. Riffe's widow and administratrix.

Peter Cave Coal Company, another coal mining company, had a mine adjoining the Wolfe Creek mine where Mr. Riffe worked, and at the time of Mr. Riffe's accident, Wolfe Creek and Peter Cave frequently shared equipment. In fact, employees of both Peter Cave and Wolfe Creek had used the end loader earlier in the day of Riffe's death. These employees had experienced brake air pressure and fuel problems with the end loader, but there is no evidence that anyone had told Mr. Riffe of these problems.

Mr. Riffe had just started his evening work shift when the accident happened. He was driving the loader up a haulage road between Peter Cave's and Wolfe Creek's mines. As he was climbing the hill in the end loader, the end loader's engine stopped, causing the loader to stop climbing and to lose steering ability. The end loader slid back down the hill, left the haulage road, and rolled over. As the end loader rolled, it crushed Mr. Riffe's chest, causing his death.

---

[21] Riffe v. International Harvester, No. 78-CI-197 (Martin Cir. Ct., Ky. June 16, 1981).

The Hough H-65-C end loader involved in Mr. Riffe's death was manufactured by International Harvester in January 1968. International Harvester sold the end loader to its franchise dealer Brandeis Machinery and Supply Corporation, and Brandeis sold the loader to Wolfe Creek Collieries on November 25, 1969.

The type of end loader in question has a known instability and rollover propensity, vulnerabilities that have been well recognized since the 1940s. Methods and structures for rollover protection had been designed and produced by heavy equipment manufacturers—including the defendant—before 1968, and at the time of Mr. Riffe's accident it was generally known that rollover protection structures (ROPS) were available. International Harvester even acknowledged in its 1973 compliance guide that it had recognized the need for ROPS in the early 1960s.

From a cost, knowledge, and technological standpoint, International Harvester, the loader manufacturer, could have easily furnished rollover protection for the model of end loader that killed Mr. Riffe. But International Harvester made no attempt to integrate any sort of rollover protection structure into model Hough H-65-C; in fact, it chose to exclude ROPS from the design. We were able to prove through industry brochures and documents and through testimony—both from safety and product integrity engineers and from the end loader's designers—that International Harvester had the technical knowledge and capability to provide rollover protection and chose not to incorporate it.

The annotation of this opening statement was provided by Roxanne Barton Conlin. Ms. Conlin, a former president of ATLA, has also served as president of the Civil Justice Foundation and of the NOW Legal Defense and Education Fund. She received her undergraduate, law, and master of public administration degrees from Drake University. Ms. Conlin has written numerous articles and has been a frequent lecturer on litigation and the civil justice system. She practices law in Des Moines, Iowa.

Opening Statement

May it please the court: Your Honor, respective attorneys, ladies and gentlemen of the jury. It's our job and responsibility at this time to tell you what the evidence will be in this case and what this case is about. Mr. Garmer and I represent Lou Riffe, who is the administratrix—or the person who qualifies upon the death of an individual to be the personal representative for his estate—for the estate of Don Riffe. This case involves the death of Lou Riffe's husband, Don. He was a father, a college graduate, a community leader, and a coal miner.

This case also involves damages that the jury may award for the death of Don Riffe. This is a serious case. Our evidence in this case will be that Don Riffe prepared himself for leadership and responsibility. At the time he was hurt, he was only beginning to realize his potential in earnings, leadership, and responsibility.

* * *

> **COMMENT:** Most commentators suggest omitting introductory remarks that explain the law, and the first two paragraphs of this opening statement are in keeping with that suggestion. No theme is discernible yet, but the beginnings of the damages argument can be ascertained. In cases such as this one where liability is problematic, emphasizing damages may be a helpful tactic. Additionally, the humanizing of the decedent here is effective, particularly given the difficulty of the case.

* * *

Don Riffe was a graduate of Inez High School and Morehead State College. He served in the army's military police for three years. He served on the Martin County Water Commission. He was a volunteer fire fighter, an editor of the *Martin County Mercury* for five years, and in 1977 he began to work as a truck driver at Wolfe Creek Collieries. The Kentucky Jaycees recognized him as the outstanding director in the state, and the Martin County Jaycees recognized him as the outstanding president in the history of that chapter.

On February 8, 1978, Don was 38 years old. He was working on the second shift at Wolfe Creek, moving an end loader from one part of the mines to another and going up an elevated roadway on a haulage road between Wolfe Creek and Peter Cave Coal Company. We'll learn what happened as we hear the evidence in this case, but first we'll learn some things that happened before Don ever got in that end loader. Earlier that day, Peter Cave Coal Company was using the same end loader, and two employees noticed that there were problems with the brakes and the air pressure. One of them has testified by deposition that you wouldn't notice those problems. You would lose the air, but you wouldn't notice it until after you started operating the end loader.

You'll hear that those brakes were not working sufficiently before Don ever got in the end loader. Peter Cave, through its employees, knew that. On an earlier shift that day, a Wolfe Creek Collieries employee had trouble with a loss of air pressure and the brakes freezing up. He had trouble with the end loader stalling, and he reported that to his foreman. Not only did he report it, but he asked his foreman to "red tag" that end loader, or take it out of operation. Nobody red tagged it, nobody took it out of service, and nobody warned Donnie Riffe of the problems with the end loader. Don Riffe had worked there for eight months, but if he had ever operated an end loader, we are not aware of it. So he was very inexperienced; that could have been the first time he ever drove an end loader.

* * *

COMMENT: The jurors begin to get a clear picture of Don Riffe as an up-and-coming young man engaged in important and useful work. There is also an effective use here of the flashback technique of starting with a critical event and describing what led up to the event. The "rule of three" is employed in connection with the problems with the end loader: "[1] Nobody red tagged it, [2] nobody took it out of service, and [3] nobody warned Donnie Riffe . . . ." Also note how Peter uses the present tense to demonstrate immediacy.

We'll talk about some things that happened about 10 years before the accident, in 1968, when this end loader was manufactured by International Harvester Company. I'm going to show you a model of an end loader. It has never been on a coal mine road, or anywhere else for that matter, other than in my briefcase. You can see it's from a five- and ten-cent store, but it's very similar to the one that's involved in this case.

* * *

> **COMMENT:** Here is an example of an extremely effective persuasive device: instead of using a scale mock-up, Peter uses a dime store toy to demonstrate the problems with the end loader.

* * *

You will hear a lot in this case about rollover protection. You'll learn that a rollover protective structure must be built into the design in order for it to serve any useful function. You can't build the front of the end loader and then later decide you're going to put a rollover protective structure on it, because the rollover protective structure has to be as strong as the foundation of the machine.

When this unit that Donnie was driving was made, it did not have a rollover protective structure on it. It had a weather cab, but there's a difference between a weather cab and a rollover protective structure. A weather cab is simply a roof, perhaps of sheet metal or something very cheap, and it is intended to protect the operator's head from falling objects and to keep the operator out of the rain. It's a weather cab, not a rollover protective device.

* * *

> **COMMENT:** Here Peter sets out the outline of the product claim in simple, straightforward, and easily understood language. He reassures the jurors—"You will hear" and "You'll learn"—that they will learn what they need to know to properly decide the case. Also in this portion of the opening statement a clear distinction is drawn between the device used and the device necessary to protect occupants in the event of a rollover.

At the time International Harvester made the end loader in 1968, they knew it was going to be used in a lot of different ways. They even made it articulated; as you can see, it hinges in the middle. Originally, these things were made as an add-on to a tractor. One part would have been the tractor, and then they added on the scoop so it could do more things. As time went on, they decided to make the end loaders hinged so they could do even more.

International Harvester knew when they made the end loaders that people would die on them because the end loaders made by other manufacturers were rolling over and the cab was not sufficient to withstand the rollover forces. The reason International Harvester didn't build in rollover protection was that no other end loader manufacturers did it either.

International Harvester knew of the need for rollover protective structures years before this model was sold. People were being killed because of a lack of rollover protective covers. The evidence will show, through International Harvester's own documents, that they were the leaders in rollover protective devices—not in 1968 when this one was sold, but in the early 1960s, long before this one was made. Yet the company chose to make this one without a rollover protective structure. The basic design required operator protection for human safety, and that's the only form of operator protection that could be designed as part of this product. The end loader was defective because it didn't have operator protection. Operator protection would have saved Don Riffe's life.

* * *

COMMENT: In a brief and persuasive fashion, Peter sets forth the manufacturer's relevant background and causal connection to Don Riffe's death. He tells the jurors that the company made a choice, that it knew the choice it made would cause people to die, that it made the choice anyway, and that Don Riffe died as a consequence of the choice it made.

* * *

This photograph shows an elevated roadway going from one part of Wolfe Creek mine to one part of Peter Cave. Don Riffe got in the end loader just minutes before this accident happened. There's a guardhouse down here. He traveled several hundred feet at the direction of his foreman to go to tram this hill. He'd gone to the bottom of the hill, started climbing up the hill, and reached about 450 feet when the end loader stopped climbing the hill. End loaders are not passenger vehicles and only one person can ride them at a time, so only Don Riffe knows what happened in that end loader, and he's not here to tell us.

We do know that earlier that day, at least four people who worked for these two companies said they were having problems with the end loader's brakes. The evidence can only be that when Don Riffe got on the end loader, he had trouble with the brakes. The engine had stalled that morning. What else can you conclude but that when he went up the hill, the end loader started backing down. When you lose your power on a hydraulic end loader like this one, you also lose your steering. So here he was on a runaway end loader coming down the hill. It went off the side of the road and came down through to the bottom of the hill. That was a Hough H-65-C International Harvester end loader. Without having a rollover protective structure over his head to protect him from this, Don Riffe had to support the weight of this end loader on his body. The death certificate said he died of a crushed chest instantly or shortly after this end loader crushed him.

* * *

> **COMMENT:** This description of how the incident occurred is conclusive because powerful word pictures and appropriate inferences drawn from the facts establish what must have occurred based on what had occurred previously in the day. The phrase "runaway end loader" is powerful, and the word picture of Don Riffe's having had "to support the weight of this end loader on his body" because of the manufacturer's failure is a crystal clear way to explain the reason for Don Riffe's death.

* * *

Don had a right to rely on his company to give him a safe job. He had a right to rely on the knowledge, the know-how, and the technology of the people who made that end loader to design, make, and sell a safe product. The proof in this case will be that neither his company nor the people who made the end loader did what he relied on them to do. He wasn't given a safe product to use, and they didn't make a product with operator's protection for him.

This case concerns the amount of responsibility that these various parties should bear as a result of this tragedy. Earlier we talked about the damages that were being sought in excess of two million dollars. That's a lot of money. I know it and you know it and everybody here knows it. But Don Riffe was 38 years old. He had a life expectancy of 35 more years, and he was only beginning to reach his potential. At the end of this case we'll talk with you about the evidence and about the damages, and you'll have an opportunity then to see if we have proved what we said we were going to prove. Thank you.

* * *

COMMENT: Peter concludes the opening statement by explaining comparative fault, conditioning the jury to the amount of damages requested, and asserting that although the amount requested is "a lot of money," the amount is justifiable and will be proven to be so. In approximately 10 minutes, he has set out the crucial facts of the case and led the jury to the inevitable conclusion that the defendant was careless and owes the widow a significant amount of money.

Chapter 3

Shackleford v. Joy Manufacturing Company

Part One—Liability

On May 15, 1981, Henry Shackleford, a coal miner, sustained severe injuries to his face and head when a continuous mining machine malfunctioned. Because of an electrical failure in the machine's remote-control system, part of the machine swung out and crushed Mr. Shackleford's head against a roof-support pillar on the wall of the mine. The case, which was brought against Joy Manufacturing Company, the manufacturer of the continuous miner, included allegations of strict liability, negligence, and a failure to warn.

Mr. Shackleford was working at an underground coal mine in Harlan County, Kentucky, when he was injured. On the day of the accident, Mr. Shackleford and several other members of his crew were working on and around a Joy 15-CM continuous miner, a self-propelled, hydraulically operated mining machine about 40 feet long and 26 inches high.

The front end of the machine had a horizontal revolving cutter drum that chipped away at the coal on the mine walls and broke it into pieces. As the drum cut into the coal, the machine funneled the resulting chunks of coal onto a conveyer belt, commonly referred to as the "boom," at the tail end of the machine. The boom conveyed the coal into shuttle cars known as "scoop buckets."

A remote-control box controlled the continuous miner through several switches that manipulated the miner's cutting heads and the boom. The remote-control box, which contained sensitive electronic circuitry, was linked by a 40-foot cord to a control box on the body of the continuous miner. In normal operation, the remote-control box's switches controlled various hydraulic functions on the machine.

Several days before Mr. Shackleford was injured, there had been a rockfall in the mine, during which part of the rock fell on the front end of the continuous miner but did not damage the electrical circuitry. On the day of the accident, Mr. Shackleford and his crew were using the mining machine to break up and move the rock from the rockfall. The men had already broken up one load of rock and loaded it into the scoop bucket and out of the mine.

Immediately before the malfunction, Mr. Shackleford was kneeling next to the crib—which was full of wood, rock, and other debris—and about three or four feet to one side of the boom. He was not operating the mining machine but was working in a 30-inch seam of coal when a fellow miner, Jack Webb, flipped the power switch on the remote-control box. The boom unexpectedly swung to the side, striking Mr. Shackleford in the face and pinning him against a pillar supporting the mine roof. According to Mr. Webb, the boom swung out totally on its own; he had not activated the electrical circuitry that would have activated the boom.

Under rule 42(b) of the Federal Rules of Civil Procedure, the trial judge bifurcated the liability and damages issues. As a result, the liability portion of the opening statement was limited to a general overview of the injury.

In products liability cases where the plaintiff has been seriously injured by the defendant's alleged negligence, it is customary for the defense to favor a bifurcated trial; the plaintiff usually wants to try the entire case at one time. Defendants favor separate trials because separate trials do not allow as much humanization of the plaintiff or description of the damages, and the jury is not as likely to find in the plaintiff's favor. However, if the plaintiff succeeds in the liability phase, the tables are turned, and the next step becomes a simple question of the amount of damages. That's what happened in this case.

The main theme in *Shackleford v. Joy Manufacturing Co.*[22] is that

---

[22] Shackleford v. Joy Mfg. Co., CA No. 82-9 (E.D. Ky. Dec. 18, 1984).

although coal mining is a tough and hazardous occupation, miners should be able to expect safe equipment. This theme is expressed in the last paragraph of the opening statement:

> There are many hazards in coal mining, yet Henry Shackleford had the right to expect a safe product in the coal mining environment. He didn't get one.

Opening Statement—Liability

Thank you, Your Honor. May it please the court, counsel, and ladies and gentlemen of the jury. A few minutes ago, you were on the prospective panel of jurors, and now you are the jury that has been selected to try this case. As the lawyers in this case, we are obligated to tell you what the case is about and what the facts are that you will hear from the witnesses who testify.

As you have already learned from the comments of the court, this is a case in which Henry Shackleford suffered a major head injury, including the loss of his left eye, while he was an employee of the Golden Glow Mining Company on May 15, 1981. We'll learn in this case about Henry Shackleford, who was a coal miner, and about a continuous mining machine, a Joy 15-CM continuous mining machine.

* * *

> **COMMENT:** As I discussed in the introductory chapter, the beginning of the opening statement is probably the most critical point in the trial.
>
> In this opening statement, I am straightforward and use everyday language. I make a conscious effort to avoid analogies like "the opening statement is like a road map" and "the opening statement is like a jigsaw puzzle, and as the case develops you'll be able to see how the various pieces fit into the puzzle." I prefer to use a direct approach and to simplify complicated or technical issues as much as possible. The road map and jigsaw puzzle references suggest that the case is complicated, and the average person is likely to be turned off by a complicated explanation.

In the next section from the opening statement, I refer the jurors to a model of the continuous miner. Because the trial was held in a mining community, some of the jurors were already familiar with the machine.

* * *

The Joy 15-CM continuous mining machine malfunctioned on May 15, 1981. Some of you may already know about how the machine works. For those of you who don't, generally these are cutting heads; they cut against the face of the coal. These are gathering chains that carry the cut coal and put it on this conveyer belt. This conveyer belt moves the coal down to here. This is the boom. This boom then dumps the coal into a shuttle car and moves it out of the coal mine.

This particular continuous miner, which was made in 1978, had a remote-control station, which is a little box. An operator would sit at the box and operate the controls on that remote-control station. I see that Joy Manufacturing Company has brought one in here, cleaned and brand-new looking. You will learn about the controls and switches on the remote-control station.

What happened on May 15, 1981? You will learn about how the 15-CM malfunctioned. The remote control is on the right side as well as sideways and is controlled by the operator at the control station. The operator turned the pump on, not the boom, while they were underground, but this boom, without being activated, swung to its left and pinned Henry Shackleford. It also struck and injured Sam Brock, who was the foreperson. That generally is what this case is about. It's about a boom on a continuous miner that swung on its own and malfunctioned. That's what happened on May 15, 1981.

* * *

COMMENT: In addition to the model I bring to court, there is a model brought by the manufacturer that is also used for reference. These items have previously been listed on the exhibit list. To capture the attention and imagination of the jurors and familiarize them with the equipment early in the case, it's a good idea to use a graphic representation of the equipment involved. Please note that I give the description of this technical and complex piece of machinery in simple, everyday words. For example, the remote-control station contains many electrical devices, but for simplicity I refer to it as "a little box."

* * *

You will also learn in this case about things that happened months and years before May 15, 1981, related to the design and manufacture of this piece of equipment by Joy Manufacturing Company.

This continuous miner weighs about 62,500 pounds. It costs somewhere around $250,000. When it left the Joy factory in June of 1978, it contained defects in its design and construction that made it dangerous for use in a coal mine environment. There were several defects. It had a built-in failure because of the components in the remote-control system. You will find out about all of the remote-control system's switches. You will learn from the evidence that the components in that remote-control system, in this little box, were not protected from moisture, humidity, shock, or vibration, all of which are present in a coal mine. Bear in mind that this machine, as big as it is here—about 38 feet long—was used in an environment where the top of the coal is as high as the jury rail right here. The coal miners who were working in that environment were working in a seam that was lower than the jury rail, on that piece of equipment, when it malfunctioned.

* * *

COMMENT: Always try to use props or reference points that give the jury a familiar point of reference. A simple but effective reference is the courtroom itself. In this opening, I bring home the confined and dangerous nature of the work to the jury with dramatic impact by saying, "The coal miners who were working in that environment were working in a seam that was lower than the *jury rail*, on that piece of equipment, when it malfunctioned."

* * *

Under that part that you see, where the operator controls the switches, there were unprotected wires that were exposed to the elements. There were no conduits, protective coverings, or moisture contact points to prevent what happened here. The signal was broken. It caused the boom to go out on its own without being activated by the operator, and the boom crushed Mr. Shackleford's head against the pillar in the coal mine. The machine was susceptible to failure. It was susceptible to mechanical breakdown. That's how it was designed.

Along with the design deficiencies in this product, the machine also had inadequate circuit breakers that could not be activated in an emergency.

The evidence will also show that Joy Manufacturing Company, according to its own advertising, is the largest manufacturer of coal mining equipment in this country. The company knew that these problems were there. It knew of malfunctioning continuous miners similar to this one. The proof will be that the company had the technology to create a better system for its electrical signals, and yet it did not warn either the operator or the people working with this machine that the machine could malfunction the way it did that day.

* * *

COMMENT: Notice the constant references I make to the giant corporation versus the individual coal miner. Despite the efforts of tort reformers to gain public sympathy for corporate defendants, most jurors still identify with the little guy.

Even though the case is bifurcated, the mechanics of injury and causation are relevant issues, hurdles the plaintiff must clear before being able to obtain a favorable verdict. As a result, it is appropriate in the previous passage to make the following reference to the injuries:

> The signal was broken. It caused the boom to go out on its own without being activated by the operator, and the boom crushed Mr. Shackleford's head against the pillar in the coal mine.

I also make references to advertising and promotion by the manufacturer. The jury members are consumers, and I can frequently establish a sense of identity by using evidence about the representations and advertising of a big manufacturer.

Additionally, I hope to develop the jurors' identification with Mr. Shackleford as a worker, a coal miner, a consumer, a father, a husband, and a citizen of the community. In a community like this one, many people's lives depend on the income derived from coal mining. As a result, jurors drawn from the community are much more likely to identify with a local coal miner than with an out-of-state manufacturer of coal mining equipment.

In this case I use descriptive brochures of the continuous miner that contain various references to the fact that Joy Manufacturing Company is the largest manufacturer of coal mining equipment in the United States. The contrast between the big corporate manufacturer and the individual coal miner who works in a rugged and unforgiving environment is a theme that bears repeating throughout the case.

* * *

We all know from reading the newspapers that a machine malfunctioning in a coal mine could mean instant disaster. This thing happened on its own. It happened instantly. Henry Shackleford and Sam Brock had no place to go. This thing was coming at them and there was no place to go.

* * *

COMMENT: This reference to "instant disaster" caused by machine malfunction is part of the overall theme. Similar themes should be evoked in any case involving a rugged or hazardous work environment. The opening statement should also be used as a prelude to the closing argument, where in this case the following argument is made:

> While the coal miner may accept certain aspects of mining as being dangerous, and some tragedies as being "acts of God," the miner should not be forced to assume the responsibility of a manufacturer who has chosen to make an unsafe product.

A distinction must be made throughout the case between the working conditions and the equipment used within those conditions. The working conditions may be dangerous, but there is no reason to combine dangerous working conditions with a dangerous product and thus invite tragic consequences. Tragedies occur frequently enough without any encouragement.

Without making an argument, I introduce the subtle theme in the opening statement that one of the objects of the lawsuit is to improve safety in the coal mines.

* * *

This machine was used to extract coal; it can extract four to eight tons per minute. Two days before the accident, the miners had been pillaring. In other words, they had been removing the roof supports and mining the coal from those to go into another entry. Those of you who don't know about mining and pillaring will learn all about it, so I won't go into any great detail.

The next day they cribbed up the roof. In other words, they put blocks up because the roof had come down on the front end of this continuous mining machine. The roof sat down across the cutting heads of the machine, and the miners were cribbing up the roof with boards cut longways and crossways so that the roof would not fall on the rest of the miners and so that they could eventually back the mining machine out.

The third day, which was May 15, Henry went to work for the early morning shift, 7 a.m. to 3 p.m. At about 7:45 a.m., he was in the vicinity of the miner. The assignments were made to him and two other coal miners, Mark Henry and Mike Lloyd, to break up a block that was up here across the front, out of the cutter, and move it out of the conveyer. He got up here—we have some sketches to show you. You can see Henry Shackleford right there. This is a little sketch showing what he was doing. [See Exhibit 1.] You see the rock coming down. Here are the cutting heads and the face of the coal. This is the rock coming across the front. This is the foreperson.

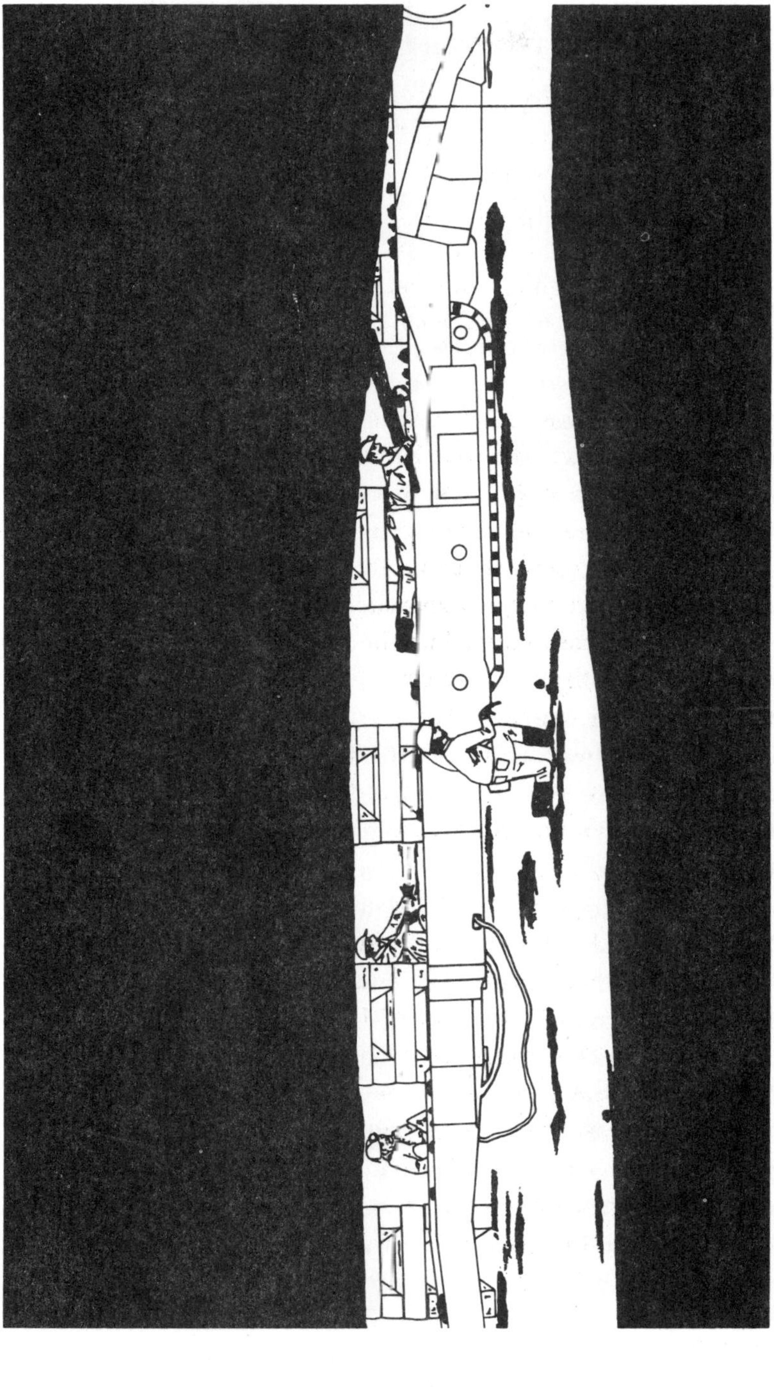

Exhibit 1: A cross-section of the mining tunnel.

They were getting the rock off to take it down this conveyer belt, to move it out on this boom. Back here there was a shuttle car that they could put the rock on. Bear in mind that this is an environment that is only as high as this jury rail, with that machine being right underneath.

This shows the rock that Henry wedged under the big rock. When he did so, they told the operator, Jack, to try the conveyer to see if it would move the rock out. Jack tried the conveyer and it worked. Henry got off. Sam Brock was already off. The other two people got off. This is a view from above. [See Exhibit 2.] This shows the big rock down at the end where the cutters are. This shows the sides of the continuous miner. [See Exhibit 3.] This shows the conveyer belt. This shows Henry; he has just gotten off. They crawled off the side and they are moving out. Here's Sam Brock. This is Jack Webb; he's over here operating the remote-control box. He's on this side of the 15–CM. The miners are on the other side of it. This is the shuttle car from which they unloaded the rocks coming off the conveyer.

When they were in this position, Jack Webb turned on the pump. The pump simply turns on the machine and gives it power. He didn't do anything with the boom. When he turned that switch, it should have just turned on the pump. He didn't touch the swing control, but this boom swung on its own, over that way. Sam Brock and Henry Shackleford were both kneeling there, about the same level as the top of that boom. It swung over and took the legs out from under Sam Brock and caught Henry Shackleford in the side of the face. [See Exhibit 4.] It crushed him against the pillar.

There is another defect. After this thing happened, people were telling Webb things like, "Bring it back, Jack." He tried, but the boom wouldn't come back. It wouldn't stop pushing, either. So they couldn't bring it back and couldn't free Henry Shackleford using the electrical system. So Jack Webb got off the box, took a crescent wrench, went over here, and broke the fittings on the hydraulic boom. [See Exhibit 5.] That released the pressure on the boom enough so that Henry could be removed. Then he and Sam were both taken out of the mine. These sketches will explain the testimony of the people who were there and will explain what caused these injuries.

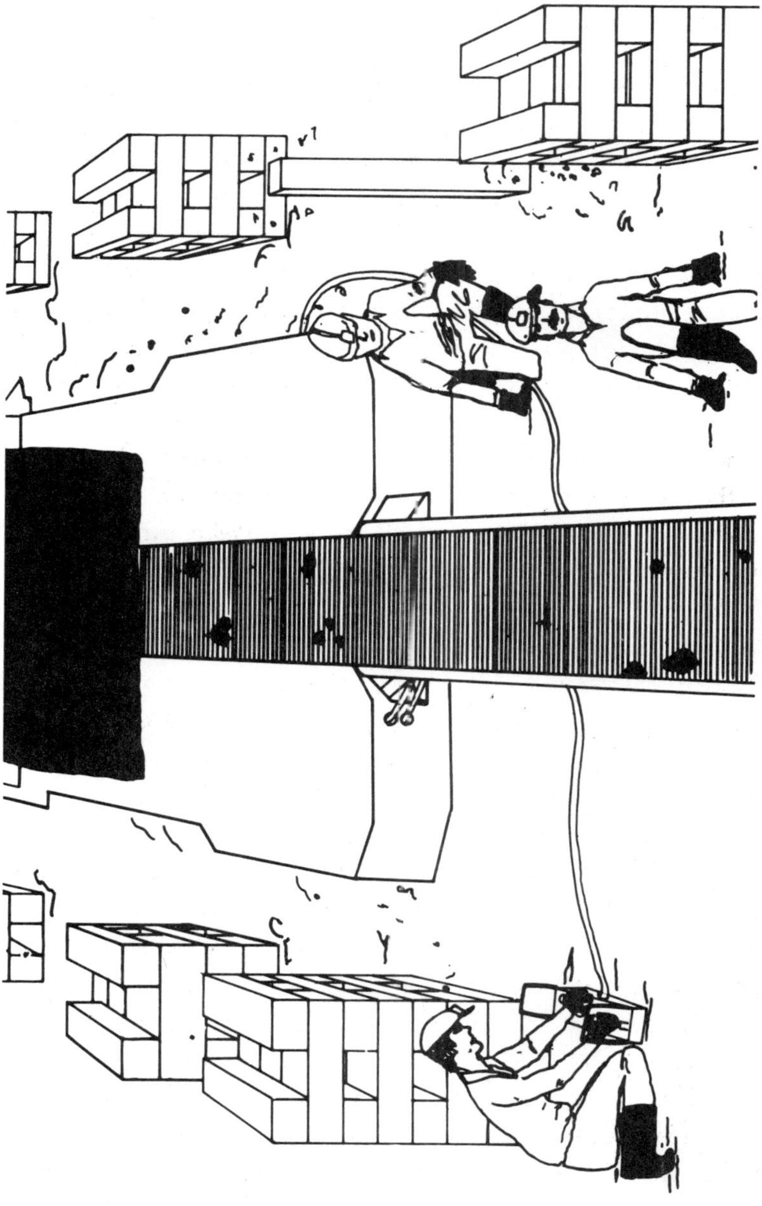

Exhibit 2: Top view of the Joy 15-CM continuous mining machine.

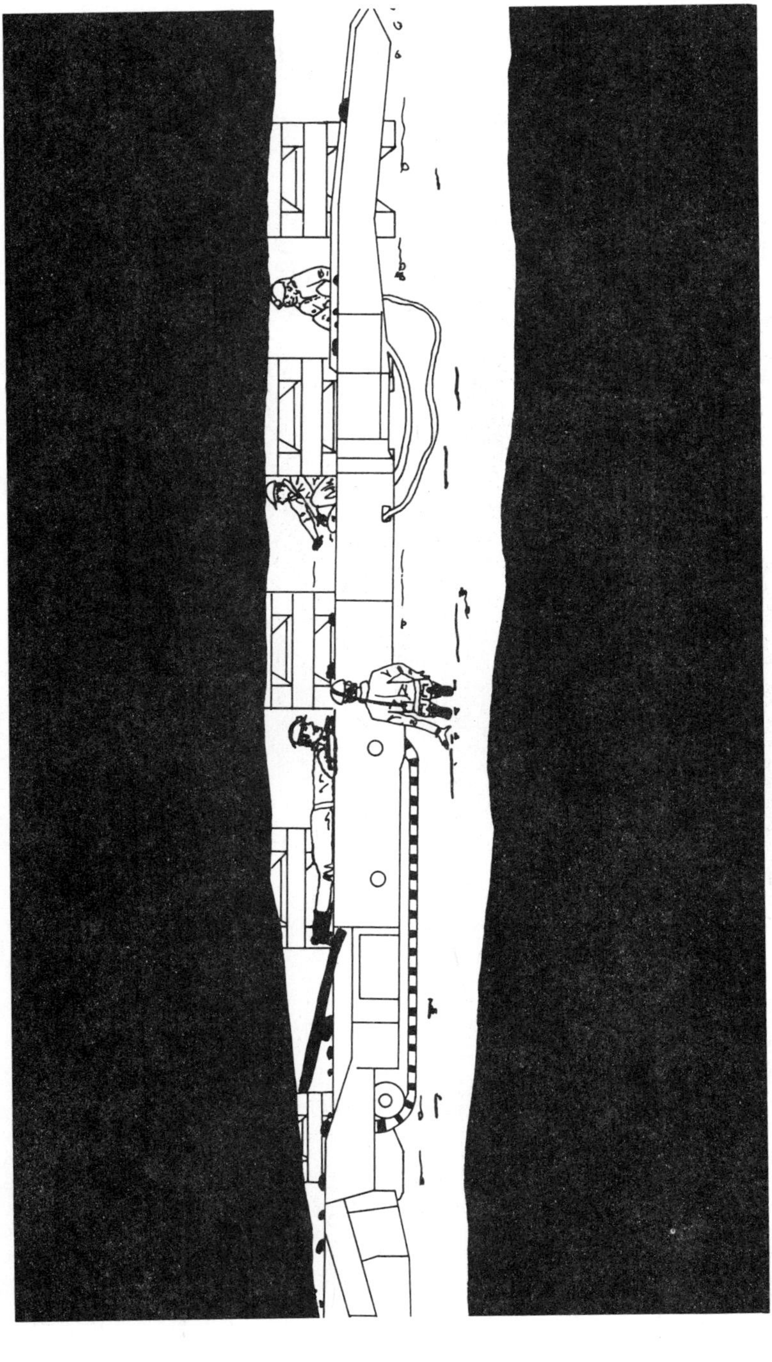

Exhibit 3: Another cross-section of the mining tunnel.

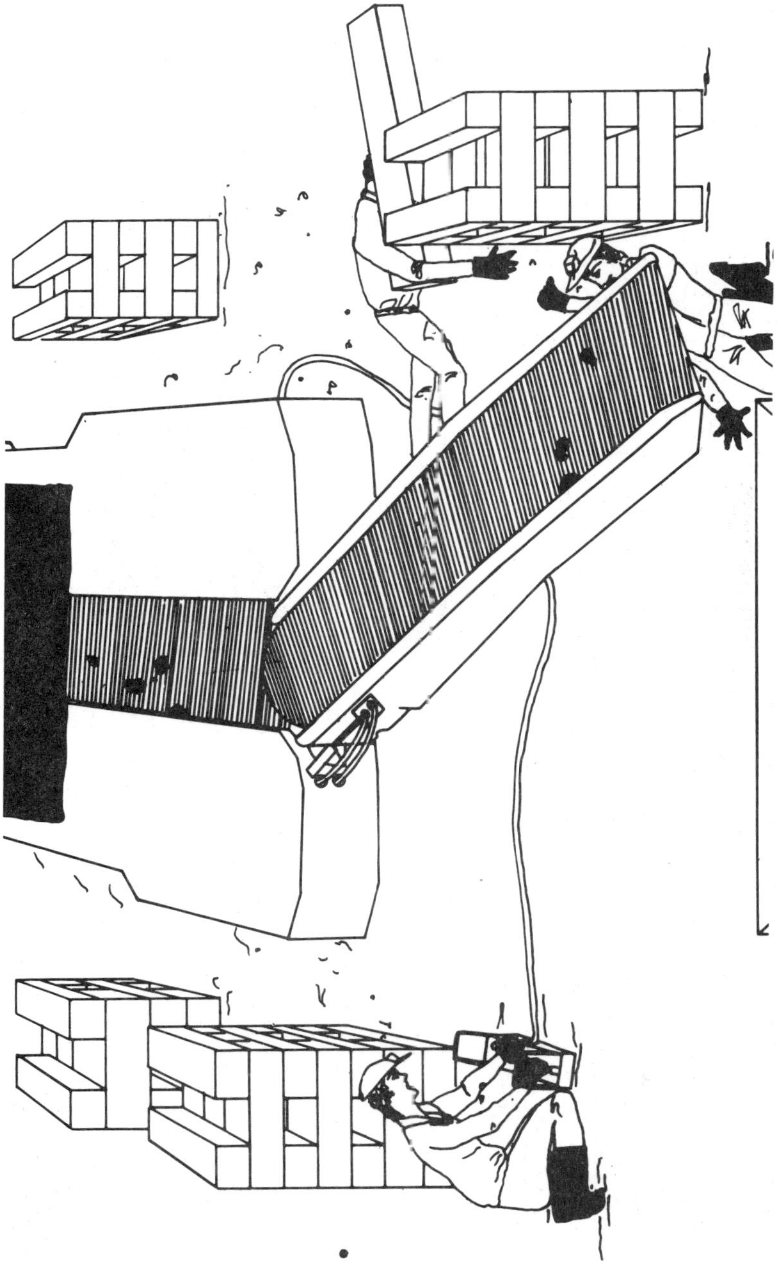

Exhibit 4: The malfunction of the Joy 15-CM boom.

Exhibit 5: The malfunction of the Joy 15-CM electrical system.

COMMENT: The sketches that are shown here are effective demonstrative techniques used to help the jury visualize the events as they developed. The sketches are not intended to be scale drawings but are simply used to illustrate the equipment and the position of the various coal miners in the underground environment. Since the section of the mine where the injuries occurred is no longer intact by the time of trial, photographs, films, or other more commonly used graphic aids are impossible to use.

Throughout this sequence of the opening statement, I tell the story in a simple, narrative form. All the facts I mention will be established without dispute, and for this reason I state them in a positive and frank manner. I avoid such language as "We expect to prove" and "We anticipate that the evidence will be"; these are much less effective and may suggest to the jury that I lack confidence in my own case.

* * *

This tragedy was caused by a machine that failed because it was unsafe and dangerous. The proof will be that the boom switch had a mechanical failure and that the pump motor signal was on, but the wiring sent the signal to the boom. The machine had a built-in propensity to fail in the environment it was in. It was not sealed. It was not airtight. It was defective. It had no adequate override whereby the operator could bring the boom back. There was no warning to anybody that this could happen or that a short within the system could cause this kind of damage.

There are many hazards in coal mining, yet Henry Shackleford had the right to expect a safe product in the coal mining environment. He didn't get one. As a result, he suffered injuries. And Joy Manufacturing has not taken the responsibility for those injuries. That's the reason we are here. Thank you.

* * *

COMMENT: The last paragraph of the opening statement is critical. You want to conclude your opening on a dramatic and high note. In this last paragraph, I express the capsulized theme of the case directly. In addition, I tell the jury that the reason for the lawsuit is not Henry Shackleford's tragedy, but the manufacturer's failure to *take the responsibility.*

Shackleford v. Joy Manufacturing Company

Part Two—Damages

The focus of the closing argument in the liability phase of this trial dealt with the manufacturer's failure to design a watertight remote-control box. As part of the machine design, bolt holes were drilled into the main chamber of the box, and the box's circuitry was not encased. Because of this, when the box was exposed to adverse environmental conditions such as dampness, the circuit breaker failed and the boom mechanism malfunctioned. Given the elements in a coal mine environment, which include moisture, humidity, shock, and vibration, this type of design was clearly inadequate and unreasonably dangerous.

In my summation for the liability portion of the trial, I used the following analogy:

> If you are a crane operator or work on a "cherry picker" machine, you get the benefit of insulation around the switch housing that protects the machine from water, dust, or dirt. Why don't coal miners deserve the same protection?

I made the following arguments in support of our position that the manufacturer was guilty of gross negligence and that punitive damages were justified:

- The manufacturer disregarded its own technology. Its own experts admitted that the manufacturer had delivered a circuitry system whereby any short would cause a total shutdown of the machine.

- The manufacturer admitted that dampness is an inherent part of the coal mine environment, that it was foreseeable that the remote-control box would be exposed to such elements, and that the technology to design a totally encased device was known and available.

- Despite such knowledge, the manufacturer made no effort to warn either the coal mine management or the workers about these specific dangers and hazards.
- The manufacturer admitted that it did not use accident statistics and injury reports to analyze field experience with its equipment.
- The person who designed the complex circuitry in the remote-control box was not an engineer.
- The manufacturer decided that it would not incorporate a fail-safe or backup system, claiming that such a system would give the workers a "false sense of security." My argument was that this was an excuse and that the manufacturer had made a design choice for profit rather than safety.

The summation of the liability portion of the trial concluded in the following manner:

> To this day, Joy Manufacturing Company and its attorneys have shown more interest in defending the lawsuit than they have in protecting coal miners.
>
> Henry Shackleford accepted the tough conditions of coal mining as part of his work environment. He was not injured by a rockfall, a roof collapse, or an "act of God." The design of this machine was a human act, and a machine malfunction should not be a risk that the coal miner has to assume.
>
> The jury has the opportunity to send a message to the manufacturer that punitive damages are justified, and in a short time maybe someone like Henry won't have to be carried out on a stretcher.
>
> Much can be done to improve safety in the coal mines. By your verdict, you have the opportunity to tell the manufacturer and others that we are the conscience of the community and we've done our part.

The jury found in the plaintiff's favor on all issues in the liability part of the case. In addition, the jury found that the manufacturer's conduct in designing a continuous mining machine with a runaway boom amounted to gross negligence and that punitive damages were justified.

Since the opening statement in the damages phase was delivered on the heels of this favorable verdict, we decided to keep the opening short. We presented the damages in a direct, straightforward manner. The theme is fairness, since the damages speak for themselves and require a substantial verdict.

Opening Statement—Damages

Ladies and gentlemen of the jury, going into the afternoon of your seventh day here, we know it has been a long time for you. The most comforting thing I can tell you right now is that the proof on the damages will be brief. But that does not mean that the damages are not substantial. You have already heard some of the facts about this case, but you haven't heard the injuries that it involves. It involves a major head injury with a fracture to Henry's facial bones, blindness in one eye, and epilepsy, and those are just some of the things that he suffered when that boom malfunctioned on May 15, 1981. The medical testimony will be through doctors who will testify on videotape: plastic surgeons, a neurosurgeon, and a psychiatrist. Their testimony will be that because of these injuries, Henry will never work again—not in the coal mines, not anywhere else. He can't be cured.

* * *

> **COMMENT:** This is the recurring theme in this case. It need not be eloquent or expressed in complicated language. The words themselves send a powerful message: "Henry will never work again—not in the coal mines, not anywhere else. He can't be cured."

* * *

You will learn from the evidence that in May of 1981, when Henry was hurt, he was 23 years old and married with one child. About two years before that, in early 1979, he had gone back to work after having been off for about 13 months. He hurt his back in the coal mine sometime in 1977 and reinjured it two or three times, and he was off. He got over his back problems, and then the miners went on strike. So as a combination of all that, he was off about 13 months. From the time he went back to work in early 1979 until this boom hit him in May of 1981, he worked full time. He supported his family. He had worked for some six years in the coal mines. He held about every job that you could hold. He had been a roof bolt operator and had also operated a scoop, shuttle cars, a continuous miner, drills, and road trucks. He was a good hard worker. You will hear evidence from Otis Belcher, who was not only Henry's supervisor, but who was also his friend off of the job.

* * *

> **COMMENT:** The jurors must be given the opportunity to identify with the plaintiff, and I try to humanize him in this sequence. I discuss Mr. Shackleford's work ethic: how, despite having suffered several back injuries in the past, he always returned to his work in the coal mines. I also mention his dedication to his family. Once again, my language is simple, and the words alone send a powerful message.

* * *

The proof will be that Henry hasn't worked in the coal mines since the boom hit him. And the evidence will be that he never will work again. In other words, he's only 27, but he's totally disabled.

After this thing happened, Henry was in the hospital in Lexington for about 15 days. In that time, doctors found he was blind in his left eye and had some loss of vision in his right. They had to rewire his entire facial structure. They rewired his jaws and sewed them back together. He lost his sense of taste and sense of smell. He had brain damage. He has had seizures ever since that time. The proof will be that he now has a life expectancy of 46 years. For damages, we'll consider the past four years and future damages for the rest of his life.

* * *

> **COMMENT:** This is a fairly simple recitation of the injuries that Mr. Shackleford suffered. No argument or flowery speech is necessary. The injuries are self-explanatory, and great impact results from simply listing them in a forthright manner. On summation, I make the following argument:

> By your verdict, you can't restore Henry's sight; you can't restore his taste; you can't restore his sense of smell; you can't take away his epileptic seizures; you can't take the wires out of his face or restore his balance and coordination. If the jury had the power to do these things, and if the jury had the power to tell Henry, "We'll make you as good as new or as good as you were before the boom pinned you against the mine rib," Henry would say, "That's great." If the jury had the power to give Henry a choice either to return to his previous condition or to take the money that is warranted by the evidence, there is no question what choice he would make. It took him 23 years to become a self-sufficient, hardworking coal miner and provider for his family and himself. It took only seconds for a runaway machine to destroy it all.

* * *

In addition, we'll ask you, the jury, to award punitive damages, based on the gross negligence that you have found in this case, that are fair and reasonable.

* * *

COMMENT: Our punitive damages argument in the closing argument also discusses the power of the jury. Some segments of the closing argument related to punitive damages include the following:

> How much does it take to get the attention of the biggest coal equipment manufacturer in the world? If one of these continuous mining machines sold for $500,000, would this be enough? This question is solely within the power of the jury. As you sit here today and as you have been here throughout the trial, you jurors have an incredible amount of power. I was just thinking about it, and in many respects you may have as much power as you will ever have. When you go to vote, you're one of thousands; when you go to a school board meeting, you may be one of hundreds. But when you sit in a case as a part of our system of justice, you're one of only six. And you have the power to right a wrong, to send a message,

> and to punish a corporate manufacturer. You also have the power to decide the amount so that this company will be punished and deterred.
>
> This case is significant in many respects. In one respect, it is significant because you have the power to give Henry Shackleford some sense of independence and some sense of pride by returning to him his financial losses. It's also significant because you have the power to protect others, and you have the power to tell this corporation that it had better fix these machines so that other coal miners don't have to suffer the same fate that Henry suffered.

* * *

All we ask for in this case is that you be fair. And we know that you will be, and that you will award fair and reasonable compensation, because this man will never work, he will never support his family; he will never do the things that he could do--hunt, fish . . . . He was doing all the work on his own house, remodeling his own house. Now he's totally disabled.

The damages in this case, ladies and gentlemen, will be very substantial. We'll put on a vocational expert who will tell you what Henry would have made if he had continued to work. And if he had continued to work, he would have made a whole lot of money that he will never make.

He needs somebody to take care of him. He's lucky to have his wife. We'll ask that you take all of this into account, and when this is over, we'll ask that you return a fair and reasonable verdict. Thank you.

* * *

> **COMMENT:** The conclusion of the opening statement repeats two basic themes: fairness and substantial damages. It also previews coming attractions and links the opening statement to the closing argument. A similar technique was frequently used by a great trial lawyer, Alfred Julien, and various examples can be found in his text on the subject of opening statements.[23]

---

[23] ALFRED S. JULIEN, OPENING STATEMENTS (1991).

Chapter 4

King v. Kayak Manufacturing Company

In 1985, Clifford King, a 35-year-old West Virginia resident, became one of some 800 Americans who suffered a broken neck from a diving injury that year. About a third of these neck injuries, including Mr. King's, were sustained in swimming pools. The most dangerous type of swimming pool is the above-ground pool. The above-ground swimming pool industry boomed in the 1950s, and the pools continue to be popular: today there are an estimated four million such pools in the country. The above-ground pool is often promoted as a "country club in your backyard." The pools are generally prefabricated and relatively inexpensive, with prices ranging from $1,000 to $6,000.

Victims of catastrophic injury from above-ground pools typically have some of the following characteristics:

- They are recreational swimmers.
- They have little or no professional training or instruction in either swimming or diving.
- They have never been in the pool before, and they don't know the depth.
- They are adults or late adolescents (since the most common above-ground pool has a uniform depth of four feet, small children make so little penetration into the pool that they are in almost no danger of injury).

- At the time they are injured, they are in an atmosphere that is relaxed, uninhibited, and free spirited; frequently beer and alcohol are present to some degree.

Clifford King fit this profile. He was a recreational swimmer who had never received professional training in diving. He had been at the pool where his injury occurred one time before the accident, but he didn't recall any specific information about the pool, including its depth. He was an adult, and on the day of his accident, a typically warm summer afternoon in August, he had drunk one beer.

Many above-ground pools are sold equipped with decks or even diving platforms. These are invitations to dive. Although the above-ground pool industry has always known about the dangers associated with use of decks and diving platforms, the warnings the industry furnishes about them are primitive. In many instances, no warnings are given.

In this case, the warning consisted of a small bumper-sticker-type decal given to the owner of the pool in which Clifford was swimming. It said, "Do not dive." There were no warnings on the sides of the pools, and there were no bottom markings. It is elementary tort law that an adequate warning must apprise the user of the severity, gravity, and extent of the danger. In addition, the manufacturer's duty to provide adequate warning extends beyond the scope of intended use, reaching into the field of foreseeable use.

Above-ground pools are heavily promoted at neighborhood malls and shopping centers, and in this case, some of the manufacturer's representatives testified that no warning stickers had been placed on the pool when it was displayed in such promotions. We requested the manufacturer's advertising and promotional material in discovery, but when responding to our request, the manufacturer failed to produce its promotional film showing several grown adults diving into the pool in much the same manner as Clifford dove. In the film, the pool is described as a "recreation center that the whole family can enjoy right outside your nearest door." We obtained a copy of the film from a lawyer who had handled a similar case, and we submitted it as evidence. Even though Clifford had not seen the film, the court ruled that the film constituted proper impeachment as it was relevant to the intended and foreseeable uses of the product.

Authorities in the field of swimming and diving have long cautioned that the average person is unaware of the risks he or she faces when diving into shallow water. The average recreational swimmer does not realize that a shallow dive may result in paralysis or quadriplegia injuries.[24]

Patricia Bobb, a trial lawyer from Chicago, annotated the opening statement I gave in *King v. Kayak Manufacturing Company.*[25] Ms. Bobb earned her undergraduate degree from St. Michael's College in Santa Fe, New Mexico, and her law degree from the University of Notre Dame. Her litigation specialty is personal injury with an emphasis on medical negligence. She currently serves on ATLA's Board of Governors, and she is both a fellow of the American College of Trial Advocacy and a member of the National Institute of Trial Advocacy's Board of Directors.

Opening Statement

May it please the court, counsel, ladies and gentlemen of the jury. The case, which you have already heard discussed, involves a catastrophic injury. It involves the quadriplegia of Clifford King on August 10, 1985, just two days after his 33rd birthday.

This case will have two basic themes. The first will be the dangerous and unsafe design, production, sale, promotion, and distribution of a swimming pool. The second theme will be the effect that the injury has had upon this man's life and the quality of living he will experience for the rest of his life.

The pool was made by Kayak Manufacturing Company, a New York corporation. Kayak Manufacturing produces and sells about 4,000 pools a year. It sounds fairly simple and straightforward. But

---

[24] *See* discussion about above-ground pools and other recreational products at EDWARD M. SWARTZ, SWARTZ PROOF OF PRODUCT DEFECT ch. 15 (1985).

[25] King v. Kayak Mfg. Co., 86-CI-766 (Monongalia Cir. Ct., Monongalia County, Morgantown, W.V. Feb. 23, 1988).

those facts are only part of the story; the rest of the story will deal with how the pool was promoted and sold. It will deal with how it was produced, assembled, and installed, its intended and expected use, the lack of safety features for its intended and expected use, and the inadequate warnings.

* * *

> **COMMENT:** The technique used here, which summarizes the case, highlights the issues to be determined, and focuses on the specific issues to be decided in the case, effectively captures the attention of the jury. In summarizing the facts and the issues in this manner, Peter immediately creates sympathy for the plaintiff and antipathy toward the impersonal, uncaring corporate defendant.

* * *

It is our responsibility to tell you what the case will be about, what we will prove, and what the facts will be. We will prove to you that Clifford King was using the pool owned by his brother-in-law, Jack Marks, in a way that the manufacturer promoted and anticipated. We will prove that the manufacturer knew for many years that people dive into four-foot, above-ground pools. And we will prove that Kayak has known for many years about the risks of paralysis to people diving into pools of this type.

* * *

> **COMMENT:** In this section of the statement, Peter anticipates the defenses to be raised in the case and defuses them by going on the offensive with a discussion of the plaintiff's conduct. He effectively points out that the plaintiff's conduct was not unusual or unexpected and shifts the blame for the accident to the defendant-manufacturer. The discussion of the knowledge of the defendant-manufacturer about the risk of paralysis gives rise to an expectation that the manufacturer should have done something to prevent injuries such as the one suffered by the plaintiff.

* * *

I'd like to tell you about Clifford's background. He is one of six children. He has a sister, Anne, who is married to Jack, his brother-in-law. He has an eighth-grade education. He was honorably discharged from the military after serving in Vietnam. There will be no claim that he was rich. In fact, he was a self-employed carpenter and was not making a lot of money at the time he was hurt. The injury occurred August 10, 1985, a Saturday afternoon.

You will hear the evidence about that day. Clifford was at his mother's home and planned to work on a truck. His brother, Robert, came by and asked him to go swimming at Jack's pool. Clifford agreed to go, and on the way they stopped to get some beer. They got either a 12-pack or two six-packs; it was not uncommon to drink beer at Jack's pool. They arrived between 1:00 and 1:30 in the afternoon. Clifford was like all of us. He took his health and the simple pleasures of life for granted. He didn't realize that day at 1:30 p.m. that he was going to spend the rest of his life in a wheelchair.

* * *

> **COMMENT:** The plaintiff is personalized here, and a picture of him as a regular guy that the jury can identify with begins to emerge. At the same time, the fact that the plaintiff was drinking at the time of his injury is necessarily revealed to the jury and its importance in the case minimized.

* * *

Let me tell you a little about Kayak, the manufacturer of this pool. The company was founded by several business people in the mid-1960s. While the pool you will see today carries the Kayak name, and the brochure carries the Kayak message, the pool wasn't designed by Kayak. In fact, Kayak doesn't employ any design engineers. You will learn that Kayak is not even a manufacturer. It is an assembler. It takes parts made by other manufacturers and puts them together. The company is a fabricator.

You will learn that the original design did not come from a patent or a blueprint. One of the Kayak officials said in a deposition, "How do you patent a box?" You will hear from the evidence that when designed and installed properly, the pool is not much more sophisticated than a box.

We will prove to you that Kayak's own promotion and marketing encouraged unsafe practices in the pool. A large adult man's diving into this pool was not only allowed, it was encouraged. Kayak's sales pitch—and they advertise in malls and in *TV Guide*—was that you could have a recreational center right outside your door. Kayak designed a pool to fit every yard and every wallet. The concept is, you don't need a country club, you don't need a local pool, you can have an above-ground pool right in your own backyard. Once they sold it, they walked away from it.

* * *

> **COMMENT:** Presenting the facts in this order again draws a contrast between the plaintiff—a regular, sympathetic guy—and the impersonal, uncaring defendant-manufacturer. The effect is to underscore the idea that all the defendant cared about was making as much money as possible. The strong language used, particularly in the last sentence, has great impact and is persuasive without being argumentative.

* * *

They left it up to the buyer, Mr. Marks in this case, and the salesperson to pick the location. "Where on your lot is the best place to put this pool? You tell us." And that's where they put it. It was left to the buyer to approve the construction and the installation. You will see where the pool is located today. Daniel Flesher, a local engineer, will tell you that Kayak used principles, procedures, and practices unacceptable in the construction industry for excavation and compaction. They did no compaction test. They only dug through one level of soil. They paid a person a flat fee to install it, $625 I think. They didn't come back after it was installed to check it for proper installation.

The result is that this pool didn't have a solid foundation. It didn't have an even bottom, and that is going to be critical when you hear what happened to Clifford King on August 10. There were variations between one depth and another depth, particularly around the center of the pool where there is a drain that sticks up about an inch and a half.

Every pool has a drain to circulate the water, filter it, and return it to the pool. You will hear that Kayak is the only above-ground pool company that uses a center drain on the bottom of the pool. Other companies use a skimmer in the wall at water level. The reason I am telling you all of this is that it is important in this case that the drain was elevated and in the center. You will hear that the basic design requires that if the drain is in the bottom, it has to be flush with the bottom. You are going to see the drain and hear testimony about the fact that it was not flush with the pool bottom. This was a great hazard. It violated the basic design of swimming pools.

* * *

> **COMMENT:** In this section, Peter clearly and simply describes the design and construction of the pool, highlighting how dangerous the pool was. The defects, as described, were not visible or detectable by persons using the pool. These facts make the failure of the defendant-manufacturer to give adequate warning of the danger even more egregious. When the extent of the hidden dangers is thus highlighted, the focus is away from the potentially harmful conduct of the plaintiff.

* * *

The expert who will talk about this and about the dangers of this pool will be Dr. Milton Gabrielsen from Plantation, Florida. He has been associated with swimming pool safety for 50 years. He has written many of the standard texts on swimming pools and safety, and he will testify to you why this pool is dangerous, why it is unsafe, and why somebody like Clifford King would have no way of knowing that. When you dive—which Kayak promotes—you suffer a real and serious risk of becoming a quadriplegic, which is what Clifford King is.

You will hear about a vinyl liner which lines both the bottom and sides of the pool. You also will see that it is a blue and white pebbly-type liner, and we will introduce evidence that this type of liner hinders rather than helps a swimmer's or diver's depth perception.

You will hear and see that there are no depth markers on the sides, the deck, the bottom, or anywhere else in the pool to tell people how much water is in the pool, or how deep it is. These markers were available and feasible at the time the pool was designed, yet Kayak simply didn't offer them as an option. Kayak didn't include them in the package, and they are not there.

You will find that there are no bottom markers or lines, nothing for the swimmer or diver to judge the depth. In this case, while the pool is advertised as being a four-foot, above-ground pool, you will hear that it is actually not that at all. It is actually only three-and-a-half feet deep.

* * *

> **COMMENT:** The plaintiff's expert is identified and his qualifications and expertise described. Once again, the "hidden" nature of the defects is underscored. The defects in the pool are described in a simple, compelling fashion. When this technique is used, the jury will be more apt to understand and be persuaded by Dr. Gabrielsen's testimony when he is called during the plaintiff's case in chief.

* * *

You will hear a lot about warnings, and you will find that there are no manufacturer's warnings on this pool about diving, about quadriplegia, or about the risk of injury from diving. You will hear that Kayak furnished the owner with two "No Diving" stickers, like bumper stickers, and then left it up to him to decide where to put the stickers. We will show that there is inadequate warning with regard to the language, the size, and the placement of the stickers. Most importantly, we will show, and we expect their witnesses to agree, that the sticker does not warn of the risk of injury and is ineffective. We will show that Kayak has known this for many years. We will also show that some of Kayak's colleagues have been designing pool warnings with symbols and red lines across them to warn of the risk of quadriplegia. But not Kayak.

This case is also about the risk of very severe injuries. As we present the evidence in this case, you are going to hear a contrast. You will hear what Kayak and the pool industry knew contrasted with what Clifford King and the public knew. Most people who suffer a severe injury—quadriplegia or paralysis—in a diving accident have no head injury at all, or only a bump or a minor bruise. Yet their necks break, their spinal cords are severed, and they suffer the most permanent injury of all, quadriplegia, with only a bruise to show. Kayak knew this. The public and Clifford King did not know this. For the average person, and specifically for Clifford King, diving into an empty four-foot pool would be risking serious injury. The untrained or recreational diver doesn't know that diving at a clear angle into a pool with four feet of water is hardly safer than diving into an empty pool. The untrained or recreational diver doesn't know, but Kayak does know, that the better the dive, the greater the risk of serious injury.

The evidence will show that the danger, the hazard, and the risk were known and have been known to Kayak for some time, yet you will find that this pool has been designed without any changes to the critical elements.

* * *

> **COMMENT:** The concept of failure to warn, particularly where the plaintiff's conduct in causing his own injury is a problem, is important for the jury to grasp in a products case. The manner in which it is discussed here not only makes it understandable, it also persuades the jury that the defendant-manufacturer's failure to adequately warn the plaintiff of the hidden defects in the pool was the true cause of the plaintiff's devastating injury. The case's theme—which contrasts the superior knowledge and responsibility of the defendant-manufacturer with that of the plaintiff—comes through loud and clear. Without being argumentative, the presentation of the facts in this fashion persuades the jury that the defendant is responsible.

* * *

These are just some of the things that the public and Clifford King didn't and wouldn't be expected to know but that Kayak and those in the business knew and would be expected to know. On the basis of that evidence, we will ask you to find at the conclusion of this case that Kayak was not only negligent in designing an unsafe product but was also willful, because despite their knowledge they showed a reckless disregard for basic safety.

* * *

COMMENT: By this point in the statement, Peter has given the jury more than enough facts to justify his request for a favorable verdict. Because the factual foundation has been so effectively presented, the jury will not be offended by this request for a particular verdict at such an early stage in the case. The use of a legal term such as "reckless disregard," which the jury will likely hear again in instructions at the end of the case, is a particularly good technique.

* * *

Mr. Marks is the owner of the pool. He is here because he is the brother-in-law of Clifford King. He participated in the design selection, not the design itself. He also participated in the selection of where the pool is. You will hear evidence about the pool's dangerous location because it is not on a firm, solid foundation. You will hear evidence that people dove in this pool, including members of Mr. Marks's family.

* * *

COMMENT: Because the pool owner is a defendant in the case, the reason for his inclusion must be acknowledged. His presence in the case is explained, and a basis for establishing some responsibility on his part is given. The manner in which this is done permits the jury to assess some relatively minimal damages against him if they want to, without taking away from the major responsibility of the defendant-manufacturer. Since the defendant-manufacturer will undoubtedly cast blame on the pool owner during the trial, it is important for the plaintiff to acknowledge this possibility without detracting from the strength of the case against the defendant-manufacturer.

* * *

I will tell you about Clifford's injury, but we won't go into it in any great length because you will hear the evidence. Let me tell you first that Clifford won't sit here throughout the trial, not because he is not interested, but because we have advised him that he shouldn't be here during the entire trial. So when he is not here, that will be the reason. We believe it would not serve any useful purpose for him to be here throughout the entire trial.

* * *

> **COMMENT:** The tactical decision has been made to keep the plaintiff out of court during the trial; if he is present, the jury may become desensitized to his catastrophic injury. Because the jurors will wonder why the plaintiff is not in the courtroom, they must be told why they will not see him.

* * *

Clifford was a recreational diver. He had no formal training. He had no experience with above-ground pools. He had been to this pool only once before, and that was the previous summer in 1984. He said he jumped in the pool that time but others were diving in the pool, too. That was the previous summer. Then on August 10, 1985, his brother picked him up; they got some beer and went over to his brother-in-law's pool. He was there for 30 minutes or so. He saw his nephew, Bobby, trying to dive and belly flopping instead, so he offered to teach him. So Clifford demonstrated a couple of dives from the end of the pool longways, and then Bobby would follow. Then Clifford moved over to the side of the pool about four feet from the edge so that he was ready to dive in and swim across to the ladder at the other side, and he will tell you that all three dives were about the same: they were shallow. They were done with arms and hands extended.

The third dive coming from the side going toward the ladder was the critical one. That is when he hit the drain in the middle of the pool. We know that he hit the drain because afterwards there was some scalp and hair stuck on the drain. He hit a solid object protruding from the bottom, and that caused his head to stick. The body would keep moving forward, but the neck is only designed to support a head weighing 12 to 14 pounds, not a body that weighs 170 pounds. The neck becomes the point of least resistance. That is what makes somebody a quadriplegic.

COMMENT: The mechanics of the plaintiff's dive and how he was injured are clearly explained. This is done because the jury must understand how the dangerous defects in the pool actually caused the injury to the plaintiff. The mechanics of the injury are presented in a graphic, horrifying way. At the same time, the plaintiff's conduct and manner of diving are presented in a way that makes them seem reasonable and predictable.

* * *

In addition to Dr. Gabrielsen from Nova University, who is one of the leading aquatic injury authorities in this country, we will hear from Kevin Filson, director of aquatics here at the university, who will testify that this pool is unreasonably dangerous. We will have expert testimony that but for the drain, the location, and the method in which it was installed, along with the other factors mentioned, these injuries would not have happened. Clifford wouldn't be here today, and you wouldn't be here today.

We know basically what the position of the other parties in this case will be, and I will comment on that very briefly. They will say that Clifford did a sailor's dive, and a sailor's dive, from what I understand, is when you keep your hands at your side and dive in head first. Ladies and gentlemen, you will hear the evidence, and Clifford will tell you that he didn't do a sailor's dive. And his brother, Robert, who came in for the trial, saw the two previous dives, although he didn't see the last one, and he will tell you that the first two were shallow dives. Clifford will tell you that he doesn't even know how to do a sailor's dive and has never done one.

You will also hear the defense tell you that he did a one-and-a-half-revolution flip from the side of the pool into a body of water four feet deep or less. Clifford will tell you that he didn't do a one-and-a-half flip. Our experts will tell you that unless you are a world-class gymnast, it is impossible to do a one-and-a-half flip into that body of water. The people Clifford talked to after the accident asked about his history and what happened; there is no mention of a sailor's dive or a flip, but you will be able to hear the evidence and make your own judgment.

COMMENT: The jury is told here that the plaintiff will present another expert who will testify that the pool was unreasonably dangerous. This reemphasizes the strength of the plaintiff's case. The manner of the plaintiff's diving is once again mentioned, and the defendant's expected counter-allegations are responded to in a matter-of-fact way that minimizes the importance of the plaintiff's conduct in the case as a whole.

* * *

The damages in this case are substantial. Clifford was at the West Virginia Medical Center for about two weeks—that was his initial care—and was treated for compression injuries, a fracture of the sixth cervical level of the neck. He was at the VA Medical Center in Richmond for about six months for active and extensive treatment and rehabilitation. Presently, he needs rehabilitative care, physical therapy, and continuous monitoring. He will need nursing care for the rest of his life, and his earning capacity has been destroyed.

Ladies and gentlemen, this is a serious and catastrophic case. As you all agreed when you were chosen, your decision is to be based on the evidence and the evidence only, and we expect that the evidence will overwhelmingly support a verdict for a very substantial amount.

* * *

COMMENT: Ending with a brief description of the catastrophic injuries to the plaintiff is compelling. It emphasizes the importance of the case to the plaintiff without going overboard to evoke the jury's sympathy. The focus is on the "catastrophic" injuries as the basis for a "substantial" award. The jury is, in effect, told that the damages will necessarily be high because of the nature of the injuries. This technique accomplishes the purpose of conditioning the jury to award big money without suggesting an amount. To suggest a specific amount before the jury has heard the evidence would be risky.

Chapter 5

Price v. Datsun, Division of Nissan Motor Corp.

This case deals with the death of a 20-month-old child following a relatively minor intersection collision. The collision took place on a four-lane highway when a 1975 Datsun model B-210 was sideswiped by another driver. The Datsun was driven by Shirley Price; her son was in the back seat. Mrs. Price was traveling at approximately the speed limit (55 miles per hour), and the other driver was traveling between 15 and 20 miles per hour. As the result of the impact, the Datsun skidded sideways and then rolled over. The child was ejected, ending up 60 feet beyond the point of impact.

The case was brought both against the driver who turned into Mrs. Price's lane of traffic and against Nissan Corporation. The case against the driver was settled before trial, so the trial ended up as a pure crashworthiness case against Nissan.[26]

I state the theme of the case early in the opening statement:

> This is a case about the life and death of a little boy who was killed when a Datsun 1975 model B-210 rolled over. The evidence will be that the car rolled over following what should have been a minor impact.

In a crashworthiness case, it is easy to get entangled in technical terms, concepts, and explanations (like "enhanced damages," "crash-

---

[26] Price v. Datsun, Division of Nissan Motor Corp., CA No. 83-138 (E.D. Ky. Apr. 14, 1988).

worthiness," or even "the second collision"). These are unnecessary and often only confuse the jury. In this opening statement, I deliberately choose not to use such terms. Instead, I state that in a foreseeable impact in which two vehicles collide at an intersection, the intended function of a vehicle is protection. I then discuss the rollover propensity of the vehicle and the vehicle's failure to perform its intended function.

Before the trial, a settlement was reached with the other driver. Since the jury was entitled to apportion its verdict, no reference to the settlement was permitted during the opening statement.

Opening Statement

May it please the court, counsel, and ladies and gentlemen of the jury. You have heard a little bit about the case in the earlier proceedings, and it is time now to tell you what evidence we will put forth as to what happened on that day in July 9, 1981. We will try to bring to you all the evidence of the people who were there, all the people who know anything about how little Kevin met his death on July 9, 1981.

We'll try to use the best taste and restraint, without any exaggerations. You will be the sole judges of the facts, and you will have to make a decision based on what you know about the facts and—you recall the oath—based on all the evidence that's presented in the courtroom.

You know this is a case about the life and death of a little boy who was killed when a Datsun 1975 model B-210 rolled over. The evidence will be that it rolled over following what should have been a minor impact. The case also involves the damages that the jury may award under the law for both the child's death and, I will tell you right now, what some of you would consider fairly minor injuries to the mother, Shirley Price. It also involves the damages that the father has suffered by reason of what the law calls loss of society and companionship of a child and loss of consortium.

* * *

COMMENT: Although Mrs. Price suffered a neck injury, the injury was healed by the time of trial, and we address this head-on in the opening statement. We minimize her injuries and the loss of consortium claim of her husband, because these claims pale in comparison to the wrongful death of the little boy.

A similar example can be found in the classic treatise written by Leonard DeCof.[27]

* * *

The theory of the case is that a manufacturer, like Nissan, that places a product on the market that is either defective or unreasonably dangerous—and in this case the evidence will be that this vehicle was unreasonably dangerous because it had what's known as a rollover propensity—must be responsible for the damages caused.

We believe that the facts and the evidence will be very clear. The collision between two vehicles on a clear summer day in July of 1981 is one of the most common types of collisions—an impact of one vehicle striking another vehicle from the side.

In fact, the evidence will be that all circumstances were typical, known, and predictable on highways and roadways in central Kentucky and around the entire country. The evidence will be that all circumstances were typical except one, and that is the fact that a car rolled over after a relatively minor impact from the side.

* * *

COMMENT: In this sequence, I'm asking the jurors to identify with the circumstances and the unfortunate victims. The images I create include those of a clear summer day and one of the most common types of collisions. I show the jurors that all of the circumstances involved are typical, known, and predictable. The only thing not typical, known, and predictable is that a well-designed vehicle would roll over after a relatively minor impact from the side.

My objective is to make the theme as clear, concise, and simple as possible. In this manner, I want to condition the jurors and create in their minds the feeling that a car should not roll over following a relatively minor impact.

---

[27] DECOF, *supra* note 9, at § 13.01.

You're going to learn about the people; you're going to learn about the product. First, let me tell you about Wally Price and his wife Shirley. Wally works at a company known as E-Systems that does electrical work at the Bluegrass Army Depot. Shirley works at the People's Commercial Bank. They have a child, Nicole, and at the time of the collision they had two children: Nicole, age four, and Kevin, who at the time was 20 months.

* * *

COMMENT: The opening statement should answer six simple questions: who, what, when, where, how, and why.

I could spend more time in discussing the "who" question with the jury, but at this point I choose to humanize Wally and Shirley Price and their children in a fairly brief manner. I also refer to them throughout the opening statement on a first-name basis, and the process of humanization continues. Note that I make no reference to "my clients" or "the plaintiffs." These figurehead references tend to dehumanize and should be scrupulously avoided.

* * *

The evidence will be that July 9, 1981, was a nice warm summer night. Wally played on a softball team, and he left home around seven o'clock to play softball. And he will tell you about seeing little Kevin, before he left, for the last time; and you're going to hear that evidence. Shirley and Kevin, around eight o'clock, left to go to her mother-in-law's to pick up the other child, Nicole, whose nickname is Nikki. It was about eight o'clock, but it was still daylight.

Shirley had a 1975 Datsun that had been bought used at the Stevenson dealership there in Winchester. It was pretty much her car. But since Wally drove a pickup truck, it also was the family car. She took it to work, she carried the children around in it, and it pretty much served as the family vehicle on family outings and things of that nature.

* * *

COMMENT: I explain the events leading to the collision in simple lay language. The use of familiar images and activities also helps the jury identify with my client.

> This section begins with the statement "The evidence will be." This is in contrast to opening statements that use such language as "We expect the evidence to be" or "We believe we will show." The latter examples suggest to the jury that you lack confidence in the case and add to the temptation to use "lawyer talk."

* * *

The road was Highway 627 north, coming out of Winchester and heading toward I-64. It is a four-lane highway. The speed limit is 55 miles per hour. You will hear evidence that there was traffic in front of Shirley, and there was traffic behind Shirley. She was traveling in the left-hand lane as she approached the intersection. And you will hear that the reason she was in that lane is because there was a turnoff up ahead where vehicles in the right-hand lane would turn off, and the traffic going straight through would be in the left-hand lane. She was going straight through.

As she approached the intersection of Early Drive, the evidence will be that she saw a white car heading in the opposite direction slowing down as if to turn.

Now let me show you the model. This would be Shirley's Datsun going north on Highway 627, which is Maple Drive. This is the intersection of Early Drive. Can everybody see? This is the intersection of Early Drive. You can see that Early Drive is a two-lane road, divided by a median, with a two-lane road in the opposite direction. Shirley in the Datsun is going north in the left-hand lane of the northbound lanes. This is the white vehicle approaching from the north.

* * *

> **COMMENT:** This reinforces the basic theme that until the collision, nothing happened that was out of the ordinary.
>
> Although I have already told the jurors about the collision and rollover, in this sequence I am walking them slowly through the events that led to the collision.
>
> The opening statement should give the jury a sense that something is about to happen.[28]

---

[28] Fred Wilkins, *Art of the Opening Statement*, in BEST OF TRIAL: PRODUCTS LIABILITY 159 (1991).

Now the evidence will be that as Shirley approached this intersection some several hundred feet away, she saw the white vehicle slowing down as if to turn. She continued; the other vehicle continued. As Shirley reached the intersection, the white car turned. Shirley swerved, and the white car impacted with the driver's side of Shirley's car. The impact with this white car was right—you can see from these photographs—at the portion of the left headlight of the white car.

Witnesses will describe the events. We will use the model; we will use some diagrams; we will probably use the police officer's diagram. These are the basic facts as to what happened at the time of the collision. Shirley will tell you what she remembers. She thought the car wouldn't go through the intersection. She remembers that she began to swerve to the right, and that's the last thing she remembers until after the collision.

Other witnesses will tell you what they saw. And the evidence will be that in no way did anything that Shirley did in the driving of that automobile cause or contribute to this accident, in terms of her being careless or doing anything wrong.

* * *

COMMENT: As you can see, the only name that has been repeatedly mentioned is Shirley's. I mention the fact that "witnesses will describe the events" and that they will tell the jury what they saw. However, the identity that I want to create is with Mrs. Price, and so I treat the other witnesses and police officers as supporting characters.

This opening statement is meant to get the listener to think about the plaintiff as a person with a name. Even in reading this opening, you should be thinking of Mrs. Price as a person. As I mentioned before, opening statements or closing arguments in which the plaintiff is referred to as "the plaintiff" or "my client" tend to dehumanize the person and trivialize the trial process.

* * *

We'll bring you the driver of an automobile who was following the white car. He was following the white car in another automobile as the white car approached and stopped. He is a postal service employee from Dayton, and he will tell you that he saw the white car, an '80 Chevrolet Chevette; the driver of that car is a lady by the name of Shelba Lynch.

He will tell you that he saw the car come down here and stop at the intersection. And he'll tell you that Shirley was coming on in this lane at the normal rate of speed for traffic on that highway and that as she got somewhere in the intersection, this car pulled into her lane. Shirley swerved to try to avoid the car, and he first thought that they had avoided contact, that there wasn't any contact at the intersection. But it turned out that they had collided. And as you saw from the pictures of the damage to the white car, it was a minor impact to the area of the left front headlight of the white car. [See Exhibits 1 and 2.]

There's a service station up here, and there will be several witnesses who were there. They also saw some of the events, and they are going to be called as witnesses. One of those heard a horn blow and tires screech. He looked up, and he saw the Datsun swerve. He'll tell you that it was traveling at an average rate of speed for that roadway. And one of the witnesses who was up at the gas station several hundred feet away says that he saw traffic both in front of and behind the Datsun that Shirley was driving.

* * *

COMMENT: In this portion of the opening statement, I emphasize the minimal damage done to the white car—"a minor impact to the area of the left front headlight."

In crashworthiness cases, "blame the driver" is one of the major defenses used by the manufacturer. For this reason, the driver's actions and her reasonable driving have to be emphasized. To that end, I again mention Mrs. Price's efforts to avoid the collision. I describe in detail how Mrs. Price was exercising reasonable care: she was in her own lane; she drove at a normal rate of speed; when the car pulled into her lane she swerved to avoid the collision; she blew her horn and slammed on her brakes. It's also significant that all this testimony will be coming from witnesses and not only from Mrs. Price.

Exhibit 1: The 1980 Chevrolet Chevette driven by Shelba Lynch.

Exhibit 2: The 1975 Datsun B-210 driven by Shirley Price.

This testimony from other witnesses about Mrs. Price's reasonable driving behavior reinforces the case, and it also significantly defuses the defense's strategy. In the absence of some other explanation for a vehicle rollover on dry, smooth pavement at relatively low speeds, the rollover propensity and stability of the vehicle become critical questions.

* * *

Now, the reason we're here. It started years earlier than 1981 at the manufacturing plant of the Nissan Corporation. The evidence in this case will be that the Nissan (Datsun), before it had one mile on it, left the Nissan factory with a defect. And that defect was that the car tips or rolls over under conditions when it shouldn't. That's what the evidence in this case will be. It's one very basic defect that contributed to and caused this rollover.

* * *

COMMENT: Frequently in the opening statement, I want to plant a thought that will be revisited again in summation. The most basic element of a products liability case is that the product contained a defect at the time it was manufactured. Although I don't do so in this opening statement, I sometimes make an analogy to a time bomb. The time bomb is present throughout the life of the product, and at some point the bomb explodes, resulting in catastrophic damage. The only uncertainties are the time of detonation and the identity of the victims. In this case, I draw this analogy in the closing argument.

In addition, I discuss with the jury the "reason we're here." I develop this thought further as the opening statement progresses and also in the closing argument.

* * *

We will bring you an expert named John Noettl from Arizona, and you're going to hear about the experience he has had in the area of rollover characteristics, rollover propensity; he has a master of science degree in engineering. You're going to hear a lot of terms, and it's going to sound complicated, but the principles are fairly simple.

The term "stability ratio" will be used. And you're going to hear things about "track width," which means the tracks of the wheels under the automobile; "center of gravity," at what point or how high on the vehicle is the center of gravity; and "wheel base." Those terms will be used to explain a formula; and the formula establishes what a car's stability ratio is, or how easy it is for it to roll over. And Mr. Noettl will tell you that in terms of stability ratio the Datsun B-210 is at or near the bottom among passenger cars of that vintage.

* * *

> **COMMENT:** The stability ratio of a vehicle is based on a mathematical formula, and it's a fairly technical concept. I think it's important to introduce the subject in general terms and to discuss with the jury the components of the "stability ratio." The main point I want to make is that this vehicle is "at or near the bottom" of the range, considering similar vehicles of the same vintage. This shows the jurors that the car did not have a safe design and was unreasonably dangerous.

* * *

The evidence will be that this was a catastrophic event that need not and should not have happened. The evidence will be about this built-in propensity to roll over. You're going to hear some evidence to the effect that on impact, this white car went on through and wound up on the other side of the road, that Shirley's car then skidded sideways—you will hear different estimates from the witnesses at the service station—skidded sideways, and then the driver's side came over the passenger's side. The vehicle rolled over.

* * *

> **COMMENT:** The model is used during this sequence. This allows the jury to visualize the position of the vehicle, to understand the location of the witnesses, and to actually see the car roll over.

* * *

There will be some testimony that it was more than one roll, and some witnesses will testify that they don't really remember how many rolls it was. At the very least, you're going to hear that it rolled over one or more times. And in the course of the rollover, this little child was thrown out of the vehicle.

One of the witnesses, the postal employee who was behind Ms. Lynch in the Chevette, will describe to you the roll. He will tell you he couldn't believe the way it rolled, and he will describe it for you. The witness who was at the service station thought he saw an arm come out, and it turned out to be the arm of the child.

* * *

COMMENT: As you can tell, there is a difference of opinion between the witnesses as to the number of times the vehicle rolled over. Because no one was expecting it to happen or was looking out for it, this inconsistency is understandable.

At this point, I don't want to take sides on the issue; I simply tell the jury that different accounts will be presented. However, I point out that all of the witnesses agreed on the one crucial fact—that the vehicle did roll over. The most graphic testimony will be from the witness who saw an arm come out of the car during the rollover; the arm will turn out to have been the arm of little Kevin Price.

I present this in simple shirtsleeve English, and it is so gripping that no elaboration is necessary.

* * *

Mr. Noettl, who will testify as an expert, will tell you that the car had an extremely low threshold for rollover for a passenger vehicle and that a vehicle that rolls over following a minor impact is unreasonably dangerous.

And you're going to hear from all witnesses here that Mrs. Price's speed was certainly within the traveling speed of vehicles on that roadway, which is called an expressway and finally leads to I-64 about 500 feet from the intersection.

* * *

COMMENT: Every part of the case, including the opening

> statement, should logically fit into the overall theme.[29] This last section is not just a preview of the expected testimony of the expert; it is a reinforcement of the theme expressed at the beginning: A vehicle that rolls over following a minor impact is unreasonably dangerous. In addition, the expert's testimony forces the hand of the defense. The defense attorney tells the jury in his opening statement that the "impact was unique and involved a freak set of circumstances." He also argues that "this was a very serious accident." But the evidence that will be presented, along with the common sense of the jurors, will not support the defense's theory.

* * *

The evidence will be that in a matter of seconds, a routine, pleasant, and enjoyable Thursday drive became a scene of shock, terror, and unexpected tragedy. You will hear how Shirley, after her car came to rest, got out of the car where it was rolled over some 240 feet from the intersection, and how she had to look for her little son, who was some 80 feet back toward the point of impact. These events are not easy to digest, but you'll hear them.

Without going into too much detail here, I'll tell you that the rescue squad came, the police came, and Kevin was taken to the Clark County Hospital, where he was pronounced dead at 8:50 p.m., something less than an hour from the time of the collision.

* * *

> **COMMENT:** Simplicity often has a far greater impact on the jury than flowery speech and numerous adjectives. The jurors are taken back to the scene, and they are led to imagine what it's like for a mother to walk down a highway and find her small child critically injured.

---

[29] *See* FREDRIC G. LEVIN, EFFECTIVE OPENING STATEMENTS: THE ATTORNEY'S MASTER KEY TO COURTROOM VICTORY 111 (1983). *See also* BERTRAM G. WARSHAW, TRIAL MASTERS: A HANDBOOK OF STRATEGIES & TECHNIQUES THAT WIN CASES (1984).

Nissan's position in this case will be that this car did not have a dangerous rollover propensity. It will bring you several experts who will testify to those facts. Very simply, the evidence we will introduce to meet that claim is the evidence of what happened out there on the night of July 9, 1981. The evidence will be that no matter how many experts you bring in, a vehicle that rolls over following a minor impact has an unreasonable rollover propensity.

* * *

> **COMMENT:** There are various ways to address the defenses that will be raised in a case, but it is critical that you address them during the opening statement. However, since the time allotted is usually limited, you should limit the time you spend discussing the defense's position.[30]
>
> It's also important to keep the jury focused on your presentation. For this reason, I don't suggest to the jury what the defense may say during its opening statement. That would detract from the positive approach that is required to keep the jury on your side.

* * *

And Nissan's expert who has testified by deposition will also say that Shirley contributed in some way because she didn't have the child in a child's seat. The evidence will be that she did have the child in a child's seat.

You're going to find that the evidence will be that she had that child's seat in the car; there was a bucket seat, and she had the lap belt of the car strapped around the seat, and she had the child sitting in the seat. And that metal bar that goes around the front was cushioned at the time. It is not cushioned now, but it was cushioned at the time. The only thing she didn't do was strap the hooks of the seat into the hooks on the child's seat. But she did have the seat in the car, anchored by the car's seat belt.

She'll tell you why she did that, and she'll tell you that she felt she was being very safe with her son, as she had been with her

---

30 *See* discussion at DECOF, *supra* note 9, at § 1.19.

daughter. She felt that the bar around the front would protect her child, and she didn't expect that the car would roll over and throw the child out in this type of collision.

* * *

COMMENT: Besides being faced with the "blame the driver" defense, I also know that I will be confronted with the "blame the mother" defense. Throughout pretrial discovery, Nissan's representatives questioned Mrs. Price and the experts about this issue. They knew that they could not put any blame on her in connection with the way she drove the vehicle, so they wanted to find some other way to blame her for Kevin's death. She did everything right, except she didn't "strap the hooks of the seat into the hooks on the child's seat."

I feel that the best way to deal with this is to confront it directly. In addition, I know that this issue will be substantially watered down by the evidence in the case: we will introduce tables from the Kentucky State Police that show that in 1981, 88 percent of drivers with small children did not buckle them into child seats at all. So we are prepared to show that Mrs. Price was in the top 12 percent, providing well above "ordinary care."

In addition, the defense is relying on the causation testimony of a biomedical expert, but we show during cross-examination that the same expert had been extremely critical of the child seats on the market at the time the one in question was purchased.

* * *

The second and more difficult part of the case is what's called the damages. The issue for you will be to fix the responsibility for this rollover and then decide the enormously important question of what little Kevin's—what this little child's—life was worth, based on the law on which the court will instruct you.

* * *

COMMENT: Although the damages have not yet been discussed at great length, it is critical that this subject be addressed both at the beginning and end of the summation. In addition, damages have been alluded to at several points in between. In Kentucky, damages are based on the impairment to an individual's earning capacity. This is also true of a child who has not yet established any earning capacity. Also, notice the reference that I make to the need to "fix the responsibility for this rollover." I like to stress from the beginning that the question involves one of responsibility and that the jury has the power to fix or place responsibility where it belongs. This is more effective than statements like "our claim" or "the basis for this lawsuit."

* * *

As I told you, Shirley had a minor neck injury. We will try not to exaggerate that. She saw some doctors; she got some treatment. She will tell you about that. But her worst injury is having to live with and adjust to the mental effects of this tragedy. And Kevin's father will also tell you about his claim and the basis for it.

* * *

COMMENT: As I said earlier, this case is about the death of a child. It's important to be honest and direct with the jury, and not to appear greedy or overreaching.

* * *

At the conclusion of the case, we'll be back to talk to you again. We can only talk to you twice from this point on, now during what's called the opening statement, and at the end during closing argument. And you'll have an opportunity then to reflect on what I have said now and see if we have proved to you what I've told you we would prove. And that's an obligation that we make, that what we tell you we'll prove, we'll present evidence to prove.

* * *

COMMENT: This tactic is a calculated risk. It's a promise to the jury, and unless you are prepared to keep the promise, I would not suggest that you use this approach. In this case, we do not tell the jury anything in the opening statement that we cannot prove. Under these circumstances, we put pressure on the defense, and if the defense fails to prove any elements of its opening statement, the jury will not react favorably toward it.

* * *

We'll ask you first to fix the responsibility and to hold Nissan responsible. The design of the vehicle didn't cause the collision, but the collision didn't cause the child's death: the design of this vehicle with its unusual and unreasonably dangerous propensity to roll over is what caused the child's death.

The second thing we'll ask you to do is to place a fair and reasonable value on the life that was lost and the other injuries. And the evidence will be that that value is substantial. Thank you.

* * *

COMMENT: Several things should be noted. First, I do not ask for a specific monetary sum. As I mentioned in the introductory chapter of this book, there is a difference of opinion among trial lawyers on this subject. Because in this trial I was not able to conduct voir dire with the jurors, I felt it would be better to ease them into the damages that would be presented. For this reason I take a fairly low-key approach on this subject. Certainly, a compelling argument can be made to the contrary.

In addition, I again stress the concept of "fixing the responsibility."

Most importantly, I emphasize the fact that the design of the vehicle didn't cause the collision, but it did cause the child's death.

Crashworthiness cases are often referred to as "second collision" cases. The proof must separate the effects of the accident and the human effects on the occupants of the vehicle. In other words, the first collision in this case was caused by the driver of the white car, but the second collision, the one that killed Kevin, was caused by a defect in design. I say this without confusing the jurors with the term "second collision," and then I reiterate my theory: The design of a vehicle that rolls over following such an impact is unreasonably dangerous, and the manufacturer should be held responsible.

Chapter 6

Wallace v. Harley Hotels, Inc.

Bill Wallace was an elevator maintenance worker who was seriously injured when he was crushed between the top of the elevator and the top of the elevator shaft at the Harley Hotel in Lexington, Kentucky, on January 24, 1980. He died on February 12, 1980, as a result of complications from the original injuries.

At the time Mr. Wallace was hurt, he was working for Schindler-Haughton Elevator Company, a Cincinnati elevator service firm that had a contract to service the Harley Hotel in Lexington. On January 24, 1980, Robert Hensley, the chief engineer for the Harley Hotel, requested service on the elevator from Mr. Wallace's employer, and Mr. Wallace responded.

To fix the elevator, Mr. Wallace had to climb onto the roof of the elevator to check various controls located there. He asked Russell Halcomb, a Harley Hotel employee, to assist him by standing in the elevator and pushing certain buttons while he, Mr. Wallace, observed the movement of the controls on top of the elevator. When Mr. Halcomb hit one of the elevator buttons, the elevator rose to its maximum limit of travel, which is about four inches above the third floor (in other words, the floor of the elevator cab was four inches above the floor of the third floor). At the time, Mr. Wallace was on top of the elevator bending over to check the leveling switch. His back was crushed downward by the contact with the top of the elevator shaft.

On January 19, 1981, Mr. Wallace's widow, Mary Wallace, brought suit individually and as administratrix. The defendants named in the case included Harley Hotels, Inc.; Russell Halcomb; William B. Tabler, architect; and Dover Electric Company (Harley Hotels' predecessor in interest, Hospitality Motor Inn, had contracted with Tabler and Dover to design and construct the elevator shaft when the Lexington hotel was constructed in 1968). The bases of the claims against all but Halcomb were negligent construction and defective design of the elevator shaft and its components.[31]

The elevator and shaft were the subject of an inspection and investigation conducted by the Commonwealth of Kentucky and the Kentucky State Fire Marshall's Office. In the course of this investigation, it was determined that the shaft was not designed in accordance with the standards of the American National Standards Institute (ANSI). According to ANSI standards, there should have been 38 inches from the top of the elevator to the top of the elevator shaft and 30 inches between the top of the shaft and the crosshead. The affidavit of L. M. Strong, supervisor of the Kentucky State Elevator Inspectors, set forth the following violations:

- The distance between the top of the elevator and the top of the elevator shaft was 30½ inches;
- The distance between the top of the shaft and the crosshead was 22¼ inches.

Mr. Strong also stated the following in his affidavit:

> I believe it was the duty of the architect, elevator installer, and the hotel to see that there were minimum distances for clearance, and further, the failure of the architect, elevator installer, and the hotel to see that there was adequate clearance constituted the creation of an unreasonably dangerous condition which could have been avoided by adequate design or construction.

[31] Wallace v. Harley Hotels, Inc., No. 81-CI-0166 (Fayette Cir. Ct., Ky. Apr. 11, 1988) (opinion that declared Statute of Repose unconstitutional on state grounds can be found at Tabler v. Wallace, 704 S.W.2d 179 (Ky. 1985), *cert. denied*, 479 U.S. 822 (1986)).

In addition to Mr. Strong's affidavit, we filed the affidavit of a safety engineer, Raymond W. Brandt. Mr. Brandt investigated the circumstances of the occurrence and stated that Mr. Wallace's activity at the time in question was reasonably foreseeable and that the responsible parties' failure to design and construct adequate clearances between the top of the elevator and the top of the shaft created an unreasonably dangerous condition.

The theory of the case was that some critical measurements contained in the approved blueprints and shop drawings were inaccurate. On paper the measurements complied with ANSI standards. However, the measurements were never adjusted to allow for changes made during the course of the elevator's design and construction, and as a result the hoistway (the housing for the elevator cab and shaft) as built did not contain the amount of clearance specified in the blueprints and shop drawings. Consequently, the safety clearance in the finished elevator was in violation of the minimum "top car clearance" required by the elevator code in effect at the time of the accident.

In this case, a worker was injured because of the negligence of various persons and corporations involved in the design and installation of an elevator in a hotel. These included the architect who approved the plans, drawings, and final design of the elevator; the hotel chain that approved the elevator as built; and the elevator contractor who approved the drawings and final design. It was the plaintiff's position that these parties had failed to do the minimum required by the elevator industry's code.

The annotation of the opening statement of this case was provided by Howard Twiggs, a partner in the firm of Blanchard, Twiggs, Abrams & Strickland, P.A., of Raleigh, North Carolina. Mr. Twiggs received his undergraduate and law degrees from Wake Forest University. He is a former president of the North Carolina Academy of Trial Lawyers and the Wake Forest Law School Alumni Council. He has served on ATLA's Executive Committee and currently serves on its Board of Governors, and he is a member of the International Academy of Trial Lawyers and the International Society of Barristers.

Opening Statement

May it please the court and counsel, ladies and gentlemen of the jury. You've heard something about this case. You know where it happened. You know some of the facts. It is my responsibility to tell you what the facts of the case are.

* * *

COMMENT: When trial starts, the jury wants to know what the facts will be. Peter begins with a strong statement promising to tell "what the facts of the case are." The choice of words here is stronger than the usual opening in which counsel promises to tell the jury "what the evidence will show," "what the testimony will be," or—perhaps the weakest beginning—"what our contentions are."

The word "fact" is stronger than "evidence," stronger than "testimony," and 10 times stronger than "contention." In some jurisdictions it may be objectionable to "tell the facts" in opening, but a jury will not like objections in opening statements, particularly this early in opening. If opposing counsel objects and even if the objection is sustained, you should pause, thank the court for the ruling (the jury may not know if the ruling is for or against you and should be favorably impressed by your courtesy), look directly at opposing counsel and continue, "The evidence and the sworn testimony in this case will show . . ." This is a good way to punish defense attorneys when they interrupt you in opening statement or closing argument.

* * *

Bill Wallace, an elevator mechanic, had his body crushed between the top of an elevator and the top of the shaft at the Harley Hotel on January 24, 1980, sometime around 3:30 p.m., after he had worked for about six hours. He died February 12, 1980, from complications resulting from his injuries.

* * *

COMMENT: In two simple sentences, the jury is told the who, what, where, and how of the injuries that killed Bill Wallace.

This case is about an unsafe clearance for workers and others who were required, like Bill Wallace, to be on top of an elevator in the course of their work. To service this elevator, he had to ride on top of it. He was crushed between the top of the elevator and the top of the shaft. That's what this case is about.

* * *

COMMENT: Every case must have a simple theme. The theme of this case is that it is a case of "an unsafe clearance for workers" (later simplified to "a case of unsafe overhead clearance"). The theme is stated here for the first time and later repeated four times. After only 45 seconds of the opening statement, the jury knows that Mr. Wallace was required by his work to be on top of the elevator—that he *had* to be there—and that his death was caused by his being "crushed between the top of the elevator and the top of the shaft." The framework of the case is before the jury in simple, understandable, and graphic ("crushed") language.

* * *

You'll learn that Bill Wallace was a high-school graduate. He was a 42-year-old man who had an excellent employment background. He had worked for eight years in the elevator service business, the last five years with the Schindler-Haughton Elevator Company from Toledo, Ohio. The previous year, his earnings were $24,575. You will see photographs of Bill Wallace; you will learn that he was a large, robust, healthy, and industrious man. He was 6'1" and weighed 200 pounds. He was competent, qualified, responsible, and an excellent worker.

In addition to his work with his employer, he was a man with other talents and skills. For example, he could do plumbing in his home, carpentry, construction, and electrical work. He was very skilled at it. In a death case like this, a jury doesn't learn much about the personality of the person who died, because the measure of damages is the impairment to the estate. The case is pretty cut-and-dry: what is the impairment by reason of the loss of earning capacity. You will learn about Bill Wallace—his background, his employment, the way he did his work, his abilities, and his skills. What you do learn about him will be all good.

* * *

COMMENT: In awarding damages, the jurors want to know what type of person was injured or killed. A good person, a person the jurors like, who has a family they identify with, will be rewarded when the jurors answer the ultimate question of damages. Since the victim in this case was exceptionally good—a hard worker, skilled, responsible—Peter talks about him first and then goes on to fault and negligence. He leads with strength because, as a practical matter, it takes a lesser degree of negligence to find fault when the money will be awarded to a good man. The final sentence summarizing Mr. Wallace is classic. "What you do learn about him will be all good."

* * *

On the day this happened, almost eight years ago today, Wallace worked for six hours on various elevator problems. You will hear that the elevator wasn't leveling. When it reached a floor, it stopped either above or below the floor. There's some testimony that there were vibration and other problems, and he'd been working on it. His employer, the Schindler-Haughton Elevator Company, sent him down alone from their Cincinnati office. He came at the company's direction, as Harley Hotel requested, to service their elevator.

Some time in the middle of the afternoon, at about 2:30 p.m., he was still working on the leveling switches, which are on top of the elevator. He asked the hotel to give him somebody to push the button inside the elevator so that he could be above, where he could manipulate the leveling switch. I believe that Dover Elevator Company's attorney will bring in some switches, and I'm glad that they will, because you'll be able to see what he was doing. You'll also see that he had to look down between the cab and the wall to see whether it was leveling. He was concentrating on the switches and on the opening between the elevator and the hoistway.

COMMENT: The story of how Mr. Wallace was killed now comes into focus: he was on the job, where he had been sent at the request of the hotel. A hotel employee pushed the button that resulted in Mr. Wallace's death. At the time the accident happened, Mr. Wallace was concentrating on looking down.

* * *

Two people were there; one was Bill Wallace, and he's not going to be able to tell his story. The other person was Russell Halcomb, the man the Harley Hotel assigned to push the buttons on the inside of the elevator. You will learn these facts, and you will see from a model, from photographs, and from other means what Bill Wallace had to do and how he had to do it. You'll hear that the car was either on the second floor or somewhere between floors two and three. This was a three-story hydraulic elevator at the back of the hotel. [See Exhibit 1.] This is the back of the hotel. You're looking at the glass-walled elevator, designed so that people on the outside can watch the people in the elevator go up and down. At the time it was designed, around 1968, a lot of hotels put in glass-walled elevators, and this was one of them. The passengers could see the countryside around them as they went up. In this photo, this is the ground level, this is the second floor, and this is the third floor. There's some machinery inside, and this entire housing is called the hoistway. You can see a little elevation on top of the elevator. See the little extrusion through the top? That is an overhead. You will hear it referred to as a penthouse. It will become a critical area in this particular case.

* * *

COMMENT: Every effective opening statement combines show and tell. Here Peter begins to show photographs to the jury using a story telling style: "you will learn," "you're looking at," and "you will hear."

The model or photographs of the accident scene that you use in your opening statement will be the first and probably the dominant exhibit in your case. You should use the same model or photographs in depositions and list

Exhibit 1: The Harley Hotel's three-story hydraulic elevator.

them in your pretrial order. Always tell the judge in advance which demonstrative evidence you plan to use in opening statement.

* * *

This is a photograph taken from the roof. [See Exhibit 2.] Now, you can see this penthouse, which is what people in the elevator trade call it. It's not a penthouse to me. I had always thought of a penthouse as something plush at the top of a hotel. But in the elevator trade it's called a penthouse because it is above the roof. It's about the height of one concrete block.

This is a picture of what Bill Wallace saw when looking down. These railings are called a crosshead. They go across the top of the elevator, and they also form a sling around the elevator. The crosshead in this case is very critical because it is the point from which an overhead clearance is determined. I told you this was a case of an unsafe overhead clearance.

This is the light, and this was the only light they had from the top of the elevator to the top of the shaft. [See Exhibit 3.] These are some control buttons. You'll hear about them. Bill Wallace had to kneel on this crosshead to work on these switches and to look down the side of the elevator.

* * *

COMMENT: The suspense continues as the jurors are shown a photograph of a dimly lighted, overhead clearance at the top of the shaft, the "penthouse," with its clearance "one concrete block" in height. The theme of the case is again repeated, and the jury is told that Mr. Wallace had to kneel and look down to do his job as the elevator was going up. The details of the case emerge in a steady flow, vividly and effectively presented and easily understood by the jurors.

* * *

This is a photograph taken from the second floor, looking up toward the roof. [See Exhibit 4.] As you can see, the roof is a corrugated material. This is what he was crushed up against when he struck the roof.

You will hear that Mr. Halcomb was pushing the buttons as Bill

Exhibit 2: The elevator's "penthouse."

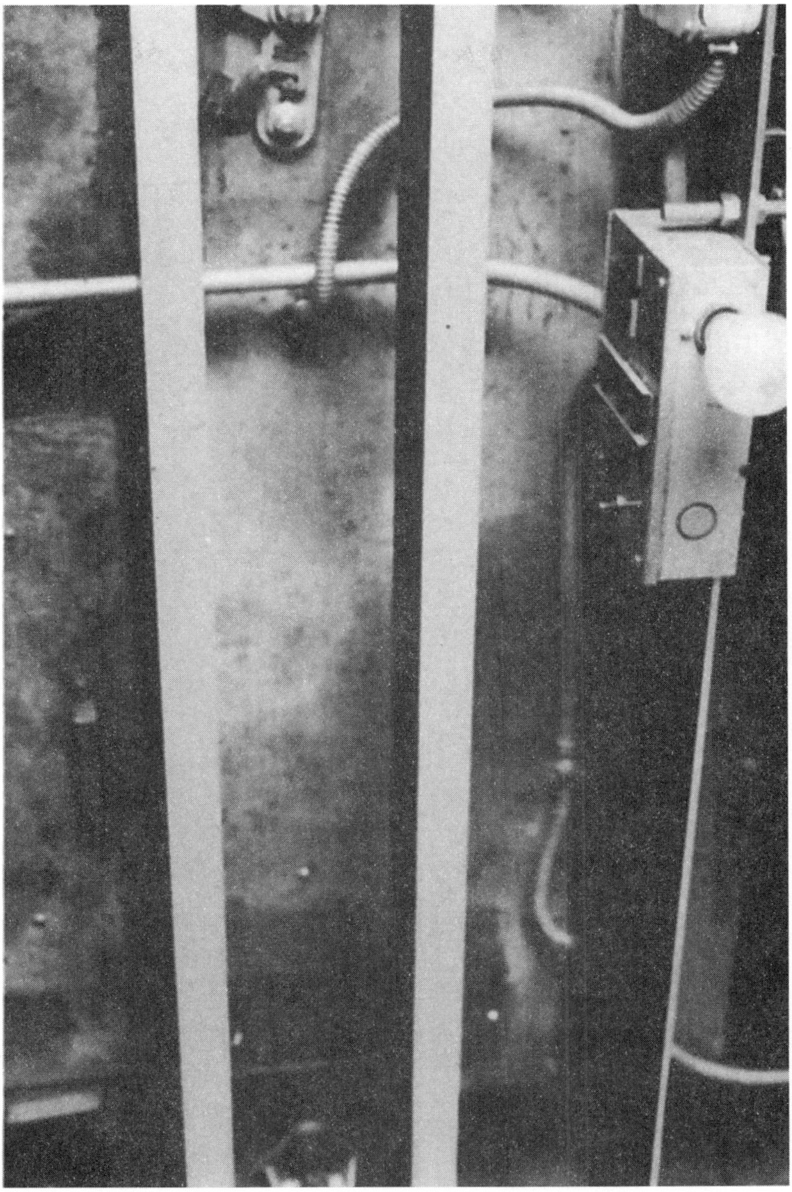

Exhibit 3: The view to the side of the elevator shaft.

Exhibit 4: The view looking up the elevator shaft from the second floor.

Wallace told him to, or at least he thought he was. Mr. Halcomb said in his deposition, and I assume he'll say the same thing here today, that he thought he got on at the second floor. In all fairness, he may have been somewhat confused because he at that time said he didn't know that the elevator had three stories. In any event, he'll say he thought he got on at two. He'll also say that Bill Wallace was on top of the elevator and told him to push a button. Whether or not he told him to push two or three will be discussed later because there's some confusion about it, but Mr. Halcomb pushed a button.

The elevator continued up to the third floor but didn't stop there; it continued up past the third-floor landing. It kept going until it reached the maximum limit of its travel, four and one-eighth inches above the third-floor landing. While Bill Wallace was operating and checking the leveling switch on this elevator, which traveled 100 feet per minute, he became aware that the elevator was going up and tried to use a stop switch. But he was unable to stop the elevator. When the elevator reached its maximum limit of travel, four and one-eighth inches above the third-floor landing, he, being a large man, was crushed up against the roof of the elevator shaft.

The evidence will show that there were 22 inches in that opening—which is the critical area of measurement—from the top of the crosshead to the top of the shaft. Twenty-two inches is a critical measurement in this case. Dr. George Gumbert, an orthopedic surgeon, will testify by deposition that Bill Wallace suffered an end-on compression. His back was crushed against the roof and his body was forced down, causing a complete collapse of both of his legs.

* * *

COMMENT: In discussing the testimony of the only living eyewitness to the accident, who is an employee of the defendant, Peter describes him as "confused." Then the eyewitness's testimony is restricted to the content of his deposition testimony by the wording of this part of the opening: "I assume he'll say the same thing here today [that he said in his deposition]."

The feeling of helplessness that Bill Wallace must have felt is graphically presented here by the description of the elevator's traveling at "100 feet per minute" (it almost sounds like 100 miles per hour) and of Bill's trying to stop it but being unable to do so before being "crushed up against the roof of the elevator shaft."

* * *

After being crushed, he was still able to lower the elevator to the second floor. A rescue squad was called. He was found, still conscious, lying across the crosshead. He was taken to Good Samaritan Hospital and treated by several specialists: Dr. George Gumbert and Dr. Brooks Morgan, both orthopedists, and Dr. Edwin Neibert, a vascular surgeon. They determined that he had a severe crushing injury to both legs, resulting in fractures of the tibia, which is the leg bone between the ankle and the kneecap.

His circulatory system was damaged—capillaries, veins, arteries. The blood vessels in his left leg were severely damaged, which compromised, or shut off, circulation to that leg. He went through surgery. The circulation problem could not be corrected, and his left leg was cut off. This was on February 3, 1980, about 10 days after he was injured. He continued to have complications and finally got a blood clot, lung congestion, and a brain abscess. Though he had the best medical care, he died February 12, 1980—19 days after the initial injury.

The evidence and the facts in this case will be that this was a death that should not have happened. This was a case of an unsafe clearance. The evidence in this case will be that rather than a clearance zone, a danger zone was created.

* * *

COMMENT: Pain and suffering prior to death is compensable only if the victim experienced them while conscious, so Peter notes here that Mr. Wallace was conscious when he received the "crushing" injuries. Additionally, Peter describes the injuries in lay terms: the tibia is "the leg bone between the ankle and kneecap," the "circulatory system" is "capillaries, veins, arteries," and Bill's left leg is "cut off," not amputated. Then themes are repeated, as "a case of an unsafe clearance" and "a death that should not have happened."

> Peter uses the vivid analogy "rather than a clearance zone, a danger zone was created"; he could have added "a death zone was created."

* * *

In the next several days, you'll look into the circumstances surrounding the design and construction of this elevator, of this shaftway, in 1968 and 1969, at this hotel. Some things are going to be clearly presented to you. This information is not hindsight, but what was known to these people, experts in their field, in 1968 and long before 1968.

We will prove that in an elevator like this one, the minimum depth of a pit where people might work is very important for those who design, install, and maintain elevators. Clearance, or headroom, above the elevator has been a concern since shortly after the turn of the century for those who design, install, and maintain elevators.

* * *

> **COMMENT:** Here, the opening statement anticipates the defense's arguments and deals with them: "this information is not hindsight" and "the minimum depth [of clearance] . . . has been a concern since . . . the turn of the century."

* * *

You'll hear about an elevator code. The operating rule in this industry and in this case is that the code governs unless local rules are stricter. In 1969, Kentucky had not adopted any stricter rules, so the code applied. You will hear, and we will prove to you, that people being caught between an elevator and a shaft has been a matter of serious concern for many years to people who design and install elevators. It is known that it is generally serious or fatal.

* * *

> **COMMENT:** Since the case is a violation of the elevator code—and the jurors are told that the code is the "operating rule" in the industry, that "the code governs," that clearance between the elevator and the shaft is "a matter of serious concern," and that insufficient clearance can result in an accident that can cause death—the code here becomes a yardstick for the jury to use in measuring negligence in the case.

We will prove that the need for safety clearance to lessen or eliminate the danger of a repair person being crushed is the very reason that these rules were established. I told you about the 22-inch space that Bill Wallace had above the elevator from the crosshead to the shaft. For this elevator, and for all elevators for that matter, the requirement at that time was six inches greater. This is a rough sketch. It's not to scale; it's simply a rough sketch to illustrate the point I'm making. This is an elevator. This is the crosshead in red. This line represents the 22 inches between the top of the crosshead and the top of the roof. This gray line represents the six inches of clearance that were required but that the elevator didn't have. Those six inches were the difference between life and death.

You're going to see a lot of drawings, specifications, blueprints, and all kinds of things. Several things are going to be pretty clear to you. The drawings for this project called for the measurement I've just given you. They called for five inches of over-travel. As I've told you, they had approximately four and one-eighth inches of over-travel. The blueprints called for five inches over-travel once the elevator reached the landing of the third floor, meaning the elevator could go five inches higher. Their own drawings called for five inches over-travel and two feet between the crosshead and the roof. In other words, their own drawings called for 29 inches. They had 22.

* * *

COMMENT: The defense is apparently going to defend by saying that the variance at the top of the shaft was minimal, only six or seven inches. Here it is shown, though, that this difference of six or seven inches is the difference between life and death.

* * *

What Bill Wallace was doing was reasonable and foreseeable and proper. Dover Elevator Company has brought in as a party Bill Wallace's employer, Schindler-Haughton Elevator Company. You'll learn from witnesses that he was sent by them to do the work requested by the Harley Hotel. The working conditions were confining. You'll learn that the leveling switch is controlled from the top, and that to watch the elevator level, you must kneel on the crosshead and look down the shaftway as Bill Wallace was doing.

There were no warnings on this job about the low overhead, the danger of the low roof. This, too, was an unsafe practice. It's our responsibility to tell you what each party failed to do, and what our evidence is, and what the facts are in that respect. Dover Elevator Company has a dual role in this case. They're here because they manufactured the elevator. They're also here because Martin A. Cedar Corporation, a Louisville elevator company, installed the elevator in 1968, and Dover later bought out Martin A. Cedar. So Dover is both the manufacturer and the installer of the elevator. They became the elevator contractor because when they bought Martin A. Cedar, they bought Cedar's assets and liabilities. So they stand in the shoes of Martin A. Cedar Company.

With regard to Martin A. Cedar and Dover, the proof will be that at the time of installation, this elevator was installed without the minimum overhead clearance. They failed to inspect the shaft before and after installation, or, if they did inspect it, they allowed it to remain in an unsafe condition, and it did not meet the minimum safety requirements required by code and by the industry's minimum safety practices. Cedar's construction mechanic had the specific responsibility of insuring that the hoistway complied with the drawings. And the hoistway did not comply with the drawings in terms of the minimum clearance above the elevator.

It was Cedar's responsibility to verify that all dimensions complied with the code. Yet they installed an elevator without an adequate clearance or any warning. I have described to you the distances when the elevator was flush with the third floor. When the floor of the elevator was flush with the third-floor landing, there was a space of 22 inches from the top of the elevator to the top of the roof, as opposed to the required 28 inches. When the elevator went to its overrun, beyond its limit of travel, the worker only had 18 inches from the top of the crosshead to the top of the roof. Those will be the parameters that you'll hear about in this case. That will be the inside of this penthouse where he was pinned. That'll be how much space he had above these crossheads at the top of this elevator. When the elevator was even with the floor, there were 22 inches from the top of the elevator to the top of the shaft. And when it went up to its maximum limits of travel, there were only 18 inches of space.

* * *

COMMENT: The opening now moves to the negligence of each defendant, separately stated. First, the Dover Elevator Company gave no warnings about low clearance and danger. Second, Dover both installed and manufactured the elevator and therefore had the "responsibility to verify" that the provisions of the code were met and the "responsibility of insuring" that the hoistway complied with the drawings. Although the jury in this case will know that there is insurance, "responsibility of insuring" is an excellent choice of words.

* * *

The second party in this case is the architectural firm. Much of their work dealt with hotels; they worked for several chains. I believe they worked for the Hilton chain, the Hospitality Inn chain, and now the Harley chain. They did the drawings and the specifications. There may be some difference of opinion between the architect and some of the other defendants about whose duty it was to follow which code or which drawing. Our evidence will be that they all had the duty to install this elevator and to maintain it with sufficient clearance for people who might be working on top of it.

Bill Wallace had a right to be there. He had a duty to be there. He was assigned to be there. The specifications for the project said that the elevator should comply with the code. The duty of making sure there was compliance was that of the architects as well as the others. That elevator did not comply with the drawings that required minimum clearance. The design of the elevator and the shaftway was a responsibility of Tabler, the architect, and Martin A. Cedar. There was a duty to design it so that it had a sufficient clearance.

You'll learn that after the initial project was drawn, there was a change. The initial project didn't call for a glass-walled elevator. When they put in the glass-walled elevator, they ordered it from a company called Otto Coerver Company. The dimensions for the glass-walled elevator were not identical to those on the original plan. It turned out that the glass-walled elevator was four inches taller than the one originally planned. It becomes clear that that's where they lost four of the inches from the clearance because they didn't adjust for the new measurement. The evidence will show that the architect had to know that this elevator did not have sufficient clearance. The architect, along with everybody else, either didn't see or didn't recognize the need to put a sign in there saying "low overhead," "low clearance," or "inadequate clearance." There was nothing.

* * *

COMMENT: Here, the negligence of the architectural firm is discussed. When the design plans were changed to install a larger "glass-walled elevator," the architects failed to adjust their measurements to compensate for the clearance needed when the elevator went to the top of the shaft.

* * *

The third party, the hotel, had final approval over the cab change. They have, by their own contract, and by the prevailing safety practice, the ultimate responsibility for complying with minimum safety standards, minimum clearances, and code requirements. In fact, they had a field representative whose job was to see that the project and the clearances complied with the standards. Our evidence will show that they didn't comply.

The hotel either didn't recognize or didn't see the need to warn. And the hotel allowed this condition to exist from 1969 until 1980.

I talked about Mr. Halcomb, the hotel maintenance employee, a little while ago. In his deposition he said he pushed floor two and the elevator didn't stop on two. Since the only other person who would know what happened was Bill Wallace, we may never know whether Mr. Halcomb pushed two, whether Bill Wallace controlled the elevator from above and made it go to three, or whether the elevator went up on its own. But you know the result. Bill Wallace was pinned, crushed, and literally sandwiched in that inadequate clearance.

* * *

COMMENT: Finally, the negligence of the hotel is covered. The hotel had the "ultimate responsibility" of meeting the code to see that there was adequate clearance, and its employee pushed the button of the elevator that resulted in Bill Wallace's being crushed to death.

* * *

Ladies and gentlemen, in conclusion, this will be a case of a worker who placed his life and trust with experts, with specialists. He didn't ask them to do the most, to build an elevator with eight feet of clearance above, but only to do the least, the very minimum. The evidence will show that they didn't do it. And the result was the unnecessary and untimely death of a man in the prime of his life, with significant damages to his estate. That will be the proof that we will present. Thank you.

* * *

COMMENT: The closing of this opening statement is short, direct, and strong, ending with the confident assertion, "That will be the proof that we will present."

Overall, this opening statement is simple, complete, and persuasive. The jury has been told what the facts will be but not promised more than can be delivered. The opening focuses on negligence and leaves the question of damages to the closing argument, which I think is wise, because I am convinced that before the evidence is in and liability is determined, jurors are generally not ready to accept a plea in opening statement for millions of dollars.

Primacy has been used to advantage in this opening statement, and if polling had been done after the case, I believe it would have shown that the case was decided in favor of Bill Wallace after the opening statement.

Chapter 7

Smith v. Humana of Kentucky, Inc.

Smith v. Humana of Kentucky, Inc.[32] was a medical negligence case that went to trial 13 years after the birth of Shannon Smith, son of the plaintiffs, Fred and Linda Smith. At birth, the fetus was in a breech position, and the treating obstetricians decided to deliver the baby vaginally rather than by cesarean section. During delivery, the baby's head was caught in the cervix, and as one of the doctors pulled the head out, he caused a fracture of the left parietal bone in the baby's skull. As a direct result of this birth injury, Shannon suffered permanent physical and intellectual impairment.

We felt that the obstetricians' conduct departed from accepted practice in various ways, including the following:

- They failed to properly evaluate the X-ray pelvimetry films.

- They relied on an incomplete pelvimetry report in assessing Mrs. Smith's ability to vaginally deliver the fetus (the report did not comment on the shape of the mother's pelvis, the size of the infant, or the size or position of the fetal head).

---

[32] Smith v. Humana of Kentucky, Inc., No. 84-CI-01860 (Jefferson Cir. Ct., Louisville, Ky. May 17, 1988).

- They failed to advise the mother that the baby was in a breech position, explain the complications of a breech delivery, or discuss the option of a cesarean delivery.
- They failed to diagnose a disproportion between the fetus and the mother's pelvis.
- They improperly used Pitocin to augment uterine contractions, without evaluating or considering the disproportion between the fetus and the mother's pelvis.
- They failed to perform a cesarean section.
- By pulling the baby's feet through the birth canal first, the head obstetrician failed to promote full dilatation of the birth canal and thus aggravated the "trapping" of the disproportionately large unmolded fetal head.

As a result, the baby was forcibly extracted through the contracted pelvis, causing a skull fracture of the left parietal cranial bone.

I used the opening statement to develop some themes I would revisit during summation. My closing argument included the following:

> As a result of the various departures, a large baby was forced through a small pelvis, and the baby's head predictably became trapped in the cervix . . .
>
> We all know that children are our most precious natural resource. A poet once said that "a child is a poor man's riches." We are all familiar with the signs that caution us to "be careful, children at play" and with the skull and crossbones on various products. These and many other signs send a message: Protect and safeguard our children.
>
> Long before children run, swim, or play, there are other warning signs, the very first that our children will ever receive. These are the very reasons for frequent prenatal care and special studies, like the pelvimetry studies that we have seen in this case. Their purpose is to identify whether a mother or a baby is "high risk." The purpose of all of these studies and procedures is to signal a possible problem before birth and to alert the health-care team that this is not a routine delivery, and more than routine attention will be required.

Even the leading textbook *Williams on Obstetrics* condemned what was done in this case. You will recall that even the defense experts agreed with this portion of the leading authority.

> Allowing a vaginal delivery of a term fetus in breech is fraught with danger and the decision is the wrong one on far too many occasions.

Was a complication like a skull fracture known at the time? There is no question that it was known. Again, the Williams text taught doctors that a child that was forcibly extracted would frequently receive spoon-shaped depressions on its skull, and actual fractures, generally fatal, would frequently be the result. This little child was literally forced off the table, and the mother heard a crack where the bones in the little baby's skull fractured.

The jury returned a favorable verdict for the plaintiff in this case. The main problems involved in the case were (1) the time lapse between the date of treatment and the time of trial and (2) the fact that the child had subtle injuries. The opening statement set forth the themes in the case and established the basis for the closing argument.

The opening statement for this case was analyzed and annotated by Mary Alexander, a San Francisco trial lawyer. Ms. Alexander, who specializes in products liability and personal injury litigation, obtained her undergraduate degree from the University of Iowa, her law degree from the University of Santa Clara, and her master of public health degree from the University of California at Berkeley. Before she started her legal career, Ms. Alexander was the director of environmental health at Stanford Research Institute. She is currently vice-president of the California Trial Lawyers Association. She lectures at the University of California at Berkeley, and she has written numerous articles on the topics of law and environmental health.

Opening Statement

Counsel, ladies and gentlemen of the jury, this case is about a boy named Shannon Smith. You've heard about him already. He was 13 years old this January.

The evidence in this case will be that Shannon suffered a depressed skull fracture during birth at St. Joseph Hospital here in Louisville in January 1975. Shannon is a learning-disabled child. He suffers from a condition called static encephalopathy, which is characterized by problems with articulation, coordination, learning ability, behavior, and esotropia, a condition that has to do with the balance and movement of the eyes. He will have this impairment throughout his life.

* * *

COMMENT: The jury is most alert to what is said when the attorney first stands up. All eyes are on the speaker. Peter takes advantage of those precious few minutes and commands the jury's immediate attention by beginning his opening statement with one sentence that explains the case in a nutshell. Right out of the box, the jury knows what the case is about and what the injuries are.

Here Peter also quickly sets forth a simple and straightforward theme of a boy injured for life. He uses the word "boy"—a term that elicits sympathy—even though the plaintiff is technically a teenager. Every case should have a central theme that is easily understood. If you cannot reduce your case to a few words, you had better redefine your theme. The successful case turns on a few fundamental concepts or themes that seize the jurors' hearts and minds and provide the guidelines for the jurors to decide right and wrong.

* * *

This case is about obstetrical care and management in the delivery of this baby. The goal of the obstetric profession is to deliver the baby without injury to the mother or the child. That's true now and it was true in 1975. That goal would have been achieved with Shannon's birth if he and his mother Linda had received proper obstetrical care and management.

* * *

COMMENT: Peter turns here to the liability theme, what "this case is about." The theme of taking care of mother and child is one we all care about; the phrase "mother and child" evokes an image and makes the jury want to *protect* and *provide* for them. Peter shows what the defendants did wrong by telling the jury what the goal of the obstetric profession is—proper care. Some jurors are swayed by a need to do justice while others are moved by the need to hold wrongdoers accountable; before they can select either course, the jurors must understand the wrongdoing.

* * *

The critical time in issue on January 22, 1975, is a four-hour period between 6:40 and 10:43 p.m. Various events that occurred in that four-hour period have shaped the course of this boy's life. On January 7, Linda saw her obstetrician, Dr. Hulsman, for one of her last prenatal visits. He ordered X-rays of her pelvis called X-ray pelvimetry. The purpose of pelvimetry is to obtain pelvic dimensions of the mother: her size, shape, and the various dimensions.

* * *

COMMENT: Here Peter clearly and simply sets up the facts in a way the jury can understand, providing explanations of medical terms he uses. He talks to the jurors, not down to them. He then turns to a more detailed analysis of specific aspects of the case, beginning with the purpose of the pelvimetry test and leading to another explanation of what the defendants did wrong—they did not properly evaluate and meet the purpose of the pelvimetry.

* * *

The second purpose of X-ray pelvimetry is to find out the status of the baby: its direction, its size, and the size of its head. The purposes of the X-ray procedure, the film, and the report are critical to this case—to see if that baby would pass safely through the mother's pelvis. The normal position is headfirst. On this pelvimetry, the X-ray report showed a frank breech. In other words, the bottom, or the buttocks, were first, and the feet were up on the shoulders. So the X-ray reports told the radiologist that this was not a headfirst baby but a bottom-first baby, and that's a breech presentation.

* * *

COMMENT: Peter establishes the theme of ignored early warning signs: the pelvimetry study identified a high-risk baby and should have alerted the health-care team that this was not a routine delivery, but the doctors ignored the warning.

* * *

Now, let's look at the pelvimetry chart. You might wonder where the film is that this refers to. Well, after so many years they dispose of the films, so there is no film. You are going to see only this pelvimetry chart and the other chart. But if you look at the chart, it has Linda Smith's name, her age, her address, and the doctor's name. It also has some writing: "single fetus in a frank breech presentation. The fetus approach is term. The measurements of the pelvis are adequate and are on the attached sheet." It tells you what the measurements of the mother's pelvis are, the "actual inlet anterior-posterior." "Anterior-posterior" is a fancy expression for front to back. "Transverse" means from side to side. "Mid-pelvis" is the bony part of the pelvis. You can see those measurements, front to back, side to side, and the outlet. The radiologist concluded, "single fetus at term in breech presentation. The pelvic measurements are adequate."

Now, let's go to the next significant chart. This is a chart that was created from these figures. There's the patient's name. There's the drawing of the pelvis, and the drawing shows what the references are: from A to A, from B to B, and from C to C. A to A is the measurement for the actual inlet. The final measurement is for the mid-portion. The next measurement is for the outlet, or where the baby is going to come out.

On this chart, there are measurements for normal conditions. So the doctors compare each of these measurements of Linda's pelvis to those of a normal pelvis. The first measurement, the AP, or the inlet, which is the top of the pelvis, is two centimeters below normal. The side-to-side measurement is two-tenths of a centimeter below normal. The mid-pelvis, or the anterior-posterior, is more than one centimeter below normal. The transverse is one and a half centimeters above normal.

I want you to concentrate on these measurements because this is what this case is largely about. For the outlet, where the baby came out at the bottom, the front to back is larger than normal, but the transverse, from side to side, is three and a half centimeters below normal.

This is a significant chart because it tells you, and it should have told the doctors, that four of the six critical measurements of Linda Smith's pelvis were below normal. The chart also calls for other information, such as the shape of the inlet, and that wasn't filled out. The part about the fetal head has no information; it wasn't filled out either.

* * *

COMMENT: The charts are the heart of the case, so they receive a detailed explanation. No doubt the jurors will hear a lot about the charts throughout the case, and this portion of the opening gives them a good foundation of facts. Peter tells the jurors that these charts are significant and that the case is "largely" about them. He draws attention to the charts, which may have otherwise gone unnoticed because of their technical nature. Additionally, using a blowup of a chart is an excellent technique for keeping the jury's attention and explaining complicated information.

* * *

What you can conclude, and what the evidence will be in this case, is that the doctors would have known, if they had looked at this chart, that this mother's pelvis was smaller than normal in four of six measurements. Those measurements were all recorded on January 7, two weeks before the events of January 22. The doctors didn't know anything about the size of the baby, the size of the baby's head, or any of this other information, and they didn't know about the shape of the pelvis.

* * *

COMMENT: After explaining the charts, Peter uses the phrase "What you can conclude" to bring the jury into the decision process and make it appear that anyone would reach the conclusion that follows.

* * *

Both the recognized authorities and the doctors themselves will say that it is critical in a breech birth to know whether the baby will safely fit through the pelvis. That's absolutely essential in delivering a breech-position baby. The doctors have two patients, the mother and the baby, and they are unable to touch one of the two patients. They must know the position, posture, station, and size of the baby going into the pelvis.

* * *

COMMENT: Reminding the jury that the baby is also the doctors' patient shows that the doctors ignored the second patient. The doctors did not know the baby's size or position, information crucial to that patient's protection.

* * *

In 1975, Dr. Barnes and Dr. Hulsman were engaged in a professional corporation, and you'll learn that both participated in Linda's care. You're going to see a standard prenatal chart. It has all of the times that Linda was seen by either Dr. Barnes or Dr. Hulsman. During her prenatal course, she was seen by Dr. Hulsman on all but three occasions. The three times that Dr. Barnes saw her were marked with an "OK." All the other times she was seen by Dr. Hulsman.

The reason I'm showing you the prenatal chart is that the testimony in this case is that there was nothing irregular about her prenatal course. When she went to the hospital, her prenatal progress had been perfectly normal. There wasn't anything unusual about the entries that the doctors made on each visit, except one thing: this was a breech birth situation. While it was unusual, it was certainly something that was not totally uncommon. It happens about 3 or 4 percent of the time, and doctors are expected, and these doctors were equipped, to deal with breech birth situations. There's nothing unusual about any of these events, and Linda's prenatal course was perfectly normal.

* * *

COMMENT: Here Peter tells the jury that everything was normal with the prenatal care, which is a point the defense will surely bring out in its opening statement. In this situation, Peter mentions a weakness in his case in order to minimize the dramatic impact of the weakness's revelation.

In this section of the opening, Peter points out how

common breech births are so that the jurors understand that the plaintiff's situation was not unusual but was something all doctors should know how to handle. Since cases against physicians are always difficult, the more routine the diagnosis and procedure, the more outrageous the negligent conduct will seem to the jury.

* * *

The pelvimetry X-rays have either been destroyed or are not available. But the significant thing is that neither Dr. Barnes nor Dr. Hulsman ever read the films, and they will admit that what they did read, and apparently what they relied on, was the conclusion of the radiologist that the pelvic measurements were adequate. They knew or should have known that the pelvic measurements in and of themselves were worthless without the measurements of the baby that was going to fit into the pelvis. The evidence will be that the doctors never looked at the X-ray film that, at the very least, would have given them some of that information.

* * *

COMMENT: Here is a good clear statement of the negligence, of what the doctors "knew or should have known." The jury will hear these terms again in the jury instructions, and the language is becoming part of the theme. Since many judges will not allow you to discuss the law in opening statement, this is a way to present the principle through explanation of the facts. The phrase "The evidence will be" emphasizes that what Peter is saying is fact; this emphasis prevents an argumentative objection.

* * *

According to the chart, on January 21, 1975, Linda went to Dr. Hulsman, and he found her cervix was beginning to dilate. You're going to hear all about the female anatomy. Most of you women probably know—and most of you men will learn, like I've tried to—that there's a process called cervical dilatation, which is measured in centimeters from zero to 10. A 10 is full dilatation and indicates that the baby is ready to be delivered. On January 21, Linda was one-and-a-half centimeters, so she went home. The next day, Linda passed a mucous plug at about 3:00 p.m., and she knew that it indicated that labor was beginning. She was admitted to the hospital at 6:40 p.m. You're going to hear about what happened from that point on from witnesses who were involved in Linda's treatment.

We may call Dr. Barnes, we may call Dr. Hulsman, and we may call Nurse Jean King, because they were the people involved in the treatment. We're going to talk about the departures from standard care; we're going to talk about what they did, and compare it to what they should have done.

* * *

> **COMMENT:** Peter explains that he "may call" the doctors and nurse involved. He hasn't committed to call these witnesses, but he has left the option open; if something happens later in trial, he can decide to call them in his case.

* * *

You're going to find that at 6:40, Jean King examined Linda and at that time she was still dilated one and a half centimeters. In other words, Linda was at the same stage of labor as she was the previous day in Dr. Hulsman's office. That is the equivalent of the baby's being high in the pelvis, and it indicates that it had not yet engaged; it was the beginning stage of labor. You're going to hear from some witnesses, including the expert for Dr. Barnes, a Dr. Green, that there is a rule in obstetrics that labor should progress steadily at the rate of one and a half centimeters an hour.

The next critical event occurred sometime after 6:40 p.m. The labor had not progressed from the day before at the doctor's office. A decision was made either by Jean King, or by Dr. Barnes instructing Jean King by telephone, to accelerate the labor. So Jean King infused Pitocin intravenously into Linda's arm. Pitocin is a drug used to speed up labor under certain conditions. In this case, it was given without any medical examination by a doctor of the patient in labor. It was given without any explanation to the patient, without any consent, without the patient's having any knowledge of the reason it was being done, and without a doctor present during the course of its administration. These are all critical departures from the acceptable practice in 1975. We're not judging anybody by today's standards but by the standards in 1975.

Once the Pitocin was administered, the labor advanced very rapidly. Remember that Linda was dilated one finger—fingers are used for centimeters—or one and a half centimeters the day before, the same as when she was admitted to the hospital. Let's look at the St. Joseph Hospital labor record. At 6:40 p.m., Linda was one finger. Station, high. Breech. Admitted. Dr. Barnes notified. Going to 7:15 p.m., the record talks about administering the Pitocin. It's significant that Dr. Barnes was not present when the Pitocin was given. In fact, the first entry for Dr. Barnes is at 9:40 p.m.

* * *

> **COMMENT:** Here Peter clearly establishes that the doctor was not even present until 9:40 p.m. The defendant-doctor is cornered with his deposition, the chart, and the nurse, so the jury knows the evidence is clear. It will be difficult for defense counsel to say in opening statement or at trial that the doctor was present earlier.

* * *

Dr. Barnes has given a deposition, as has Nurse King, and so has everyone else involved, and no one says that Dr. Barnes was at the hospital before 9:40. Linda will tell you that he was not there at any time before the baby was being delivered, because she didn't see him at all in her room while she was there. At 9:40, Dr. Barnes appears on the chart. That chart will be introduced to you as the labor record.

These things are fairly technical, and I'll try not to throw too much at you because it's hard to digest it all, but the Pitocin accelerated the labor and sped this baby down the birth canal at about twice the normal rate.

* * *

> **COMMENT:** "Sped this baby" is a great phrase that the jury can understand. These words are the type that ring out in the courtroom and that the jurors will remember in the jury room. The phrase is shorthand for another theme of the case: the doctor hurried this birth without the proper evaluation.

Then Dr. Barnes appeared. He decided to administer a spinal anesthetic and to deliver the baby vaginally rather than by cesarean section. Spinal anesthesia numbs the body, so Linda could no longer participate in the pushing that was needed to expel the baby, and the baby had to be delivered mechanically by the doctors.

The baby was born vaginally, and that's where the problem came in. One of the major concerns with a breech birth and a vaginal delivery is that the baby's head can get caught in the birth canal. It has been written about, documented, and known for many years. It is caused by disproportion between the baby and the pelvis, which means the baby is too big to safely pass through the pelvis. Remember that the pelvimetry records had no information about the size of the baby. The doctors knew what the size of the pelvis was, but they knew nothing about the size of the baby.

* * *

COMMENT: This section is strong in the range and depth of information it provides about what happened to the baby. These facts make the failure to perform a cesarean section seem egregious, and the obviousness of the problem is made real to the jury.

* * *

Dr. Barnes reached up to deliver the baby in a technique called "breaking up the breech." He reached up and pulled the baby's feet through the birth canal; then the baby's bottom; then the baby's chest; and then he was going to pull the baby's head out, but the baby's head got caught in the birth canal. There's a muscle called the cervix that literally clamped on the baby's neck. Each part of the baby is progressively bigger. The feet are the smallest, then came the bottom, and then the chest. The neck is small. It's about one-third the size of the head, and the neck got caught in the cervix. The head is the largest part of the baby. Everybody will tell you that.

* * *

COMMENT: The theme of the large head trapped in the cervix is compelling and easily understood. The assertions that a breech birth is a well-known problem and that "everybody will tell you" are persuasive without being argumentative. Another theme emerges in the next paragraph—that a well-known text condemns the "breaking up the breech" practice. This theme counters an argument the defendants are sure to make—that the choice of a delivery method was a matter of judgment.

* * *

The leading authority that doctors use, the book *Williams on Obstetrics*, has condemned the technique that was used as a radical and outmoded practice. So what happened at this point? The baby's head was caught in the cervix. They had to get the baby out. They used a pair of Piper forceps, which are about 18 inches long. The doctors clamp down on the baby's skull so that the baby can be pulled, and you pull the baby out. The forceps are like large nutcrackers. Dr. Barnes pulled the baby out, and in doing that, he caused a fracture of the baby's skull. The left parietal bone was fractured. Two days later another doctor, Dr. Jelsma, was asked to elevate the fracture. He removed the depression, the fracture of the bone, that was pressing into the brain.

* * *

COMMENT: Reliance on the leading text's authority makes it clear that it is not just a lawyer's opinion that the "breaking up the breech" procedure is condemned. This masterly discussion sets up a view of what happened that will remain with the jury throughout the trial.

* * *

The events in this case include an incomplete X-ray report without any information about the baby. They include X-ray films that were not read by either of the obstetricians, despite the doctors' knowledge that this baby was in a breech position. Pitocin was ordered by the doctor without his knowledge of the adequacy of the mother's pelvis to deliver this particular baby, and without proper management. He wasn't present, in violation of established procedure.

Remember that the mother's pelvis was small in four out of six measurements. It turns out that the baby was large, so there was an eight-pound, three-ounce baby with a head larger than normal being born in a pelvis that was smaller than normal. The pelvic measurements showed that the baby's head was too big for the outlet. They knew or should have known these measurements from their own records.

A c-section was never considered, and they forced themselves into a radical delivery. Their greatest fear came about: the baby's head got caught in the birth canal, and they fractured the skull in trying to pull the baby out. Dr. Charash, who is an expert in pediatric neurology, will testify that this is a child who now has a constellation of problems related to the childbirth episode and the fracture of his skull.

* * *

> **COMMENT:** Here Peter lists all the things the defendants did wrong and summarizes the departure from accepted practice. He reviews the key facts so that it is clear what the doctors knew and what they failed to do. Listing the key complaints like this has great impact.

* * *

I can't conceive of any witness coming into this courtroom and telling you that it is appropriate to fracture a child's skull in the course of a breech delivery. In fact, every witness will tell you that it is inappropriate.

* * *

> **COMMENT:** It would be ridiculous for defense counsel to stand up and say, "It is appropriate to fracture a child's skull." This is "an anchor" that is given to the jury to defuse the defense. Here the case is boiled down to a simple issue—whether it is okay to fracture a baby's skull. We all know the answer to that.

* * *

Since this child is now 13, there will be no claim made for past medical expenses. The parents had hoped that this child would be okay. Time passed, the years went by, and the problems did not get any better; they got worse. The time to make a claim for past medical expenses is gone, but you'll be asked to consider the evidence and to consider what Shannon's future damages are, the future consequences, the future impairment, the loss of future income, and the loss of the ability to lead a normal life. And by your verdict, after you hear all the evidence, you'll be asked to determine what the quality of his life will be. Thank you.

* * *

COMMENT: Once again, Peter refers to the 13-year-old as a "child," recalling the theme of protection of mother and child. He also explains here why so much time has passed between the physicians' negligence and the lawsuit; without the explanation, the jury may believe the case has no merit because it has been so long since the negligence occurred. Finally, he tells the jurors what they will be asked to do. Since liability is obvious after the straightforward presentation given in the opening, their task will be simple: they will be asked to determine the quality of Shannon Smith's life.

Chapter 8

Sexton v. Bell Helmets, Inc.

On December 27, 1984, Chad Sexton, a 13-year-old boy, was involved in a dirt-bike accident with a friend, Jackie Boggs, on a rural blacktop road approximately eight miles outside of Grayson, Kentucky. Although Chad was wearing a helmet and the vertical impact between his helmeted head and the road surface was a minor, low-speed impact of less than 10 miles per hour, Chad suffered a closed-head injury. That injury resulted in quadriparesis, a permanent condition that severely limits the movement of the extremities.

The Bell Star III helmet Chad was wearing at the time of the accident was originally purchased for Chad's older brother. When Chad was 12, he inherited the helmet along with his brother's KZ80 dirt bike.

The Bell Star III is a "full face" helmet that completely covers the head and face. The helmet consists of two primary components: the shell and the liner. The shell is made of several layers of fiberglass material that are designed to delaminate—that is, to separate to spread and absorb the energy of impact—in an accident. The liner is made of expandable polystyrene material and is designed to collapse or crush on impact and absorb energy through its own self-destruction.

After Chad's accident, the shell and liner of his helmet were still intact and the helmet showed little evidence of impact damage. Because the liner failed to collapse and absorb the energy of the impact, the energy from the low-velocity or minor impact was transferred to Chad's head, and Chad suffered a closed-head injury.

The Star III helmet was designed in March 1980 and incorporated all of the same features as its predecessor, the Star II helmet. Both helmets were designed for use in automobile and motorcycle racing, but Chad's use of the helmet for touring and pleasure was a type of use that was certainly foreseeable at the time of the helmet's design.

The Bell Star II and Star III helmets were designed with a tough, firm, and nonresilient liner. Bell's designers knew that the same type of helmet liner would not protect against both high- and low-velocity impacts. They chose to use a liner that protected users from violent or high-velocity impacts. They realized that such a liner would not protect helmet wearers in accidents where a low-velocity impact at a relatively high acceleration was transferred to the head.

The technology that would have allowed the production of a softer and more resilient liner was known and available long before 1980, but Bell Helmets specifically chose to use a tougher liner in the design of the Bell Star III. The protection that would have been offered by a helmet with a softer liner would have offered adequate protection for a 13-year-old boy like Chad Sexton in an accident like this one.

At the time of Chad's accident, there were no specific standards applying to helmets sold for use by children. Standards that did exist at that time were minimum performance requirements that required helmets to be tested at velocities between 13 and 16 miles per hour. Bell's helmets were designed primarily to protect the average adult head and were designed around the anatomy of an average adult. Additionally, even if a manufacturer adhered to the mandatory industry standards, the standards in 1984 were minimal and a product complying with them could still be defective.

The only type of warning on the helmet was a small sticker on the inside telling the user that "no helmet can protect the wearer against all foreseeable impacts." Our leading contention in the case was that this warning was inadequate because it failed to specify the nature of the harm, the manner in which the harm should be avoided, and the foreseeable risks. We argued that Bell Helmets was liable for Chad's injury because its product failed to meet the reasonable expectations of a consumer, Mrs. Sexton. At the time Mrs. Sexton bought the helmet for Chad's brother, she did so because she thought it would protect him from a head injury. Unfortunately, the helmet failed to perform as she reasonably expected.

James S. Rogers annotated the following opening statement. Mr. Rogers is a Seattle attorney with the Law Offices of James S. Rogers. He is a graduate of the University of Washington and the University of Arizona College of Law. Mr. Rogers is a past president of the Washington State Trial Lawyers Association and a member of ATLA's Board of Governors. He served as editor-in-chief for ATLA Press's *Anatomy of a Personal Injury Lawsuit*, 3rd Edition, and has spoken at seminars for bar and trial lawyer associations throughout the country.

Opening Statement

May it please the court, counsel, and ladies and gentlemen of the jury. You have heard the background of this case, and it is now our responsibility on behalf of our clients, Chad Sexton and his parents Mary and Floyd Sexton, to tell you what our proof in this case will be.[33]

* * *

> **COMMENT:** Peter spends only two sentences on preliminary matters before getting into the heart and substance of the opening statement. Because research shows that most jurors make up their minds about liability following opening statement and because according to the principle of primacy jurors believe best what they hear first, every second of the opening statement is important and must be used effectively. Lengthy introductions of parties and other persons, descriptions of how the trial will proceed, and explanations of what an opening statement is (for example, an analogy to a jigsaw puzzle) weaken the opening statement's impact.

---

[33] Sexton v. Bell Helmets, Inc., No. 3:88-0989 (S.D. W. Va. 1989).

This is a case about Chad Sexton, who is now 18 years old. You saw him earlier today, and he will be back, but he will be absent for most of the trial.

Chad lives with his parents and his two brothers about six miles outside of Grayson, Kentucky. He does not speak, but he communicates by writing on a board. And that is how he will testify in this case. As you saw, he moves around by using a wheelchair and sometimes by using a walker.

The evidence will show that he will need physical therapy, language therapy, and care and assistance for the rest of his life. He has a normal life expectancy of about 54 years, but he will need extensive care and treatment to maintain a base existence during his life.

Until December of 1984, Chad was a healthy, athletic young boy with reasonably good grades and commendable ratings in school. Two days after Christmas, on December 27, 1984, he suffered a trauma to the head and a closed-head injury. You will hear many medical terms in this case. You will learn that Chad has a condition known as quadriparesis, or limited movement of the extremities because of a closed-head injury.

This case is also about a helmet. You will see the helmet, hear about the helmet, and learn about how helmets are made. This was a crash or a safety helmet. It was designed primarily for head protection. It failed, even though it was subjected to only a minor impact. When you hear the testimony, pay attention to the impact that occurred between the motorcycle helmet and the surface that it struck. The evidence will show that the impact was well within what the helmet was designed and intended to withstand, yet the helmet did not withstand the impact.

* * *

COMMENT: Sometimes themes of the case do not have to be explicit. Peter's dual themes in this opening statement are a badly injured boy (damages) and a defective helmet (liability). Rather than telling the jury directly that the case is about a badly injured boy, he uses word pictures to tell the story of Chad's catastrophic injury and its effect on his life, contrasting Chad's current condition with his life before the injury. Peter does all this with maximum jury impact and within the space of nine short sentences.

* * *

You will learn that this helmet was purchased about three and a half years earlier for Chad's brother Darren, and at that time Darren was 13. Darren used the helmet. Then when Chad was 12 years old, he started using it. Neither of the boys had any accidents. Neither one had experienced problems with the helmet, and nothing was wrong with it as far as they could tell.

Mrs. Sexton purchased the helmet from East End Cycle Sales. She had asked for the best helmet they had. They told her this was the best that they had; it was a Bell Star III. She will tell you that she expected reasonable protection for the head in the event of an accident. The helmet did not furnish reasonable protection during a very foreseeable impact.

* * *

COMMENT: Here Peter is familiarizing the jury with the consumer expectation standard, a frequent component of products liability law in many jurisdictions. During opening statement, it is important to get the jurors thinking in terms of the applicable legal principles on which the judge will later instruct them.

* * *

You will hear detailed description about the helmet, and you will see some blowups about the manufacturer. To simplify things, let me begin by explaining that there are basically two parts to the helmet that are critical to its design. One is the shell or the outside of the helmet. This particular helmet had a fiberglass shell, which is composed of various layers of fiberglass cloth. The purposes of the shell are to give a smooth outer surface, to resist penetration, and, most importantly, to spread energy from the impact.

The second critical part of the helmet is the liner, which is the shock-absorbing part of the helmet. It consists of expandable polystyrene or Styrofoam. The purpose of the liner is to absorb energy from the impact so that the energy is not transmitted to the wearer's head.

You will hear that the manufacturer can make that Styrofoam liner relatively thick, stiff, and tough, or it can make the liner soft and resilient.

* * *

> **COMMENT:** Peter probably uses visual aids here while giving a physical description of the helmet to the jury. Professional illustrations of the helmet's shell and liner on posterboard or transparent overlays would be effective, or perhaps a simple freehand drawing of the helmet and the liner on a blackboard or butcher paper. If professional illustrations are used, defense counsel will have to stipulate to their use—as with any demonstrative aids used during opening statement—or the court will have to give its permission.

* * *

When a person wearing a helmet hits the ground, the road, or another surface, energy is absorbed either by the helmet, the ground, or the user's brain or head. In this case, the energy from the impact was absorbed by Chad Sexton's head.

I will show you this helmet. You will see a bruising on the shell of the helmet which corresponds with the impact to Chad's skull. This shell is designed to delaminate; in other words, the layers should separate to spread and absorb the energy. This helmet did not delaminate.

The liner is designed to collapse so that it absorbs energy through its own self-destruction. You will see that the liner did not collapse and absorb the energy. The shell remained intact. The liner remained intact. Chad's skull and his head absorbed the energy from this impact.

* * *

> **COMMENT:** This preceding section clearly and simply explains how a helmet is supposed to protect the head and why it did not work in this case. It is easy to confuse the jury with technical explanations in products liability cases, but Peter is adept at conveying complex technical information in a basic, understandable way.

There was very little damage to the helmet Chad wore or to the motorcycle he rode. You will meet Jackie Boggs, the friend with whom Chad collided, and you will see Jackie's motorcycle. Very little damage was done to the motorcycle.

You will hear about what led up to this entire incident, and about why the helmet struck the ground. Chad had been at Jackie Boggs's house. The two boys were going to return to Chad's house. The boys and their families lived along a country road outside of Grayson, Kentucky, and Chad and Jackie were traveling on a small road called Little Fork Road. It is an asphalt road without stoplights or businesses, and it has very little traffic.

They had left Jackie's house and were on their way to Chad's house. About a quarter of a mile from Jackie's house, Chad looked for Jackie and didn't see him. Chad then turned around and headed back toward where they had been. Chad came over the hill at the same time Jackie was coming up the road. They collided in the straightaway.

This is an enlarged picture of the country road and the scene of the accident. As you can see, it is a narrow country road. This is the hill and curve before the straight stretch. Motorcycles like Chad's and Jackie's sometimes operate near the middle of the road.

So Chad came over this road. He was on the straightaway, looking down. Chad and Jackie collided at this point. Jackie Boggs was coming up this way. Chad was going this direction. After the impact, they both continued in the same direction that they had been going and ended up 183 feet apart. Each boy was still on his motorcycle. Each tried to regain control of his motorcycle.

Where the person in the photo is standing is where Chad landed—about eight feet off the road. After the accident, Chad's motorcycle was still on the road near the point where he had landed.

Jackie Boggs ended up in this area off the road, and his motorcycle kept going. Jackie was injured, but he suffered no head injury. Chad was injured, and he suffered a very serious head injury from this impact.

* * *

COMMENT: Some jurisdictions will not permit evidence of the plaintiff's fault (in causing the underlying accident) to be compared to evidence of the defendant's fault (in designing the defective product) in enhanced injury cases like this one. Other jurisdictions will allow the comparison. Peter focuses his opening statement on the manufacturer's fault in designing the helmet; he doesn't discuss the facts of the underlying accident until about halfway through the opening. Additionally, in his description here of the facts of the accident, he is objective and does not attribute fault to either Chad or Jackie. This keeps the fault focused on the manufacturer.

* * *

One of the defense experts in this case, Dr. Newman of Canada, will testify—if he repeats his deposition testimony—that the impact of the motorcycle helmet with the surface was not more than 10 miles per hour. We submit to you that a helmet that fails to support and protect the head in a 10-mile-per-hour collision not only fails the standards which require greater protection but also fails to provide the protection that a reasonable user would expect from a helmet.

After the collision, Jackie's mother, Chad's parents, and some other people came. Chad was still wearing his helmet. It was still fastened, still buckled together. The face shield was missing and has not yet been located. But the helmet remained on and remained fastened after the impact.

* * *

COMMENT: It is important to anticipate and discuss the defendant's major defenses during opening statement. Here Peter anticipates one of the defendant's primary defenses—that the plaintiff was not wearing the helmet at the time of the impact with the ground. By letting the jury know that there were eyewitnesses who saw Chad still wearing his helmet as he lay on the road following the accident, Peter eliminates this defense.

* * *

Chad was breathing, but he was unconscious. It took some time for the ambulance to arrive. He was taken to the Cabell Huntington Hospital where he was treated for 49 days for a closed-head injury.

Thereafter, he spent almost a month, in March of 1985, at the Cardinal Hill Hospital in Lexington, Kentucky. Since that time, he has been in and out of several hospitals.

Ladies and gentlemen, the cause of these catastrophic injuries was the crash helmet, a safety helmet that was defective and unreasonably dangerous.

* * *

COMMENT: After discussing Chad's hospitalization, Peter returns to the liability theme, tying in proximate cause and the defective helmet. He continues to interweave the dual damage and liability themes throughout the opening statement.

* * *

The other defense witness is Mr. Fisher, who is in the courtroom today. He is the product manager of Bell Helmets. He said in his deposition that he is very knowledgeable about the design of helmets and that he probably knows as much about the design of this helmet as anybody. If he repeats at trial what he said in his deposition, he will tell you he can't say why this helmet didn't prevent the head injuries.

* * *

COMMENT: You must be selective in previewing a witness's testimony and only refer during opening statement to key testimony that will be persuasive on a material issue. Here Peter focuses on one specific fact from each of the two defendant experts' expected testimony, illustrating again the importance of keeping the explanation of liability simple.

* * *

We will present expert testimony to you that the reason the helmet failed is because it was not designed for how it was being used. It was not designed for low-impact, low-velocity use. Your first reaction might be the same as mine. If it's designed for high-impact, high-velocity use, wouldn't it also protect you during a low-impact, low-velocity use? The answer is no, because the thickness and the softness of the liner determine the type of use for the helmet. Bell decided to use a tough, nonresilient, stiff liner. We will show through company documents that Bell knew, by selecting the liner in this helmet design, that a high acceleration to the head would be transmitted in a minor impact. In other words, it was a helmet that should have been sold for racing or high-velocity use, not for touring, low-impact, or low-velocity use.

We will show you Bell's promotional materials and some of their technical documents as we try this case. We will also show that Bell had the technology to design a helmet for low-impact, low-speed, and low-velocity uses, yet they did not. They sold an all-purpose helmet knowing that it protected people from high-speed, high-velocity impacts much more than it did from low-speed, low-velocity impacts. They sold the same helmet for children as they did for racers. This helmet may be adequate for high speed or racing for adults, but it is not adequate for a child, whose brain has not finished growing. They did not take that into account.

* * *

COMMENT: A risk versus utility standard, which is an element of products liability law applicable in many jurisdictions, is skillfully demonstrated here to justify the plaintiff's argument that since the risk of injury to a child was great and the difficulty of making a safer helmet minimal, Bell helmets should have made the safer helmet. At the same time, Peter discusses the manufacturer's negligence without using the word "negligence," sensitizing the jurors to the court's instructions they'll hear later in the case.

* * *

In addition to the helmet's defects, we will show that Bell also failed to warn about the helmet's limitations. They promoted it as safe for uses far beyond those for which it was safe, including uses such as those in this case.

You will hear a lot about standards in this case. The American National Standards Institute had a helmet standard, a group called the Snell Foundation had standards, and there may have been others.

When you hear the evidence about standards, bear in mind that these standards were the minimum. In other words, these standards were the least Bell or any other manufacturer had to do to sell the helmets.

Bell's literature admitted that these standards were inadequate and were exceeded by ordinary daily use of the helmets. Bear in mind also that when a manufacturer promulgates standards, it takes not this particular helmet, but a specimen model helmet, and it tests it. That helmet gets a seal, and then all of the helmets get seals. If this helmet had failed under the conditions that it failed under in this case, it would not have met any standard, even the lowest standard. It didn't meet the state of the art. Not only did the technology exist to design a helmet that would protect somebody like Chad Sexton, but Bell Helmets had this technology before this helmet was placed on the market.

* * *

COMMENT: Peter again anticipates a defense by discussing the applicable standards for motorcycle helmets. By pointing out to the jury that standards set forth minimum criteria only and inferring that the model helmet worn in the instant case was not the model helmet the manufacturer had tested in determining whether its helmets met ANSI and Snell standards, he casts doubt on the defendant's future argument that the applicable standards were met.

* * *

Ladies and gentlemen, these statements are simply an outline of what we expect to prove. When we finish this case you will have an opportunity to think about whether we have proved what I said we would prove. I submit that at the end of the case, we will have proven what we said we would. At that time we will argue to you that these damages, this closed-head injury, and this paralysis are all the result of a defective and unsafe helmet. Thank you.

* * *

COMMENT: By making a commitment to the jury during opening statement that certain facts will be proved during the course of trial and by inviting the jury to determine at the end of the case whether the commitment was met, Peter demonstrates sincerity and a strong belief in his case.

Chapter 9

Morlan v. Green River Steel Corporation

Harrell Morlan, a South Carolina man who was in his early thirties, was seriously injured while working to remove and transport contaminated waste oil from an electrical transformer at the site of the Green River Steel Corporation in Owensboro, Kentucky. At the time of his injury, Mr. Morlan was employed by U.S. Pollution Control, Inc. (USPCI), a company that collects, transports, and recycles or disposes of specialized waste products. Mr. Morlan, in addition to being a truck driver for USPCI, was also classified as a hazardous waste transformer, which means that he was trained and experienced in the retrieval and transport of hazardous wastes. He had been sent on hundreds of assignments similar to the one at Green River Steel on August 22, 1988, and his assignment on that date was routine: he had been asked to collect contaminated oil from an electrical transformer and transport it to a storage facility in Tucker, Georgia.

Green River Steel, a steel production manufacturer, has been in business since 1950. The plant shut down in January 1986 for economic reasons and reopened during the summer of 1988. There were two large electrical transformers on Green River's grounds that had been used before 1986 to control the amount of current passing to the electrical furnaces from the plant's buildings and equipment. When the plant reopened in 1988, Green River's executives and safety directors decided to bypass these transformers because they no longer played a role in controlling the current.

Although Green River's executives determined upon reopening the plant that the transformers were no longer serving their purpose, the transformers slated for removal remained in the electric pathway running from the plant's generators to its buildings and machinery. De-energizing (or turning off) the transformers would mean breaking the power connection. Green River Steel's executives considered the option of running electric cables underground to fill the gap that would be left by the inactive transformers but decided not to do so because this would have been a long and expensive process. Instead, Green River bypassed the transformers by means of connections within junction boxes on top of the transformers. These junction boxes, known as lightning arrestors, effectively bridged the gap left by the inactive transformers. This meant that Green River Steel could maintain its connection to its generators even after de-energizing the transformers. However, even though the transformers themselves were not energized when Harrell Morlan arrived at the plant, the lightning arrestors on top of the transformers were still energized.

At the time Green River was making these decisions, the Environmental Protection Agency had enacted regulations concerning the removal of toxic waste, and because these transformers contained PCB-insulating oils—a toxic waste product—the oils had to be removed. Harrell Morlan's employer, USPCI, was retained by Green River Steel to extract, transport, and dispose of the contaminated fuels. The contract documents that describe the agreement between Green River Steel and USPCI specify that the "Transformers are to be de-energized and made accessible to our tractor trailer vacuum unit."

On August 22, 1988, Mr. Morlan and a co-worker from USPCI, Ferman Cail, arrived at the Green River Steel plant site in two tanker trucks, prepared to carry out their assignment.

On arriving at the Green River Steel plant, Mr. Morlan and his fellow driver were assured several times by various Green River Steel employees that the transformers were de-energized and that "all the power was off to the transformers." At one point, Mr. Morlan and Green River Steel's environmental director climbed a ladder to the top of the transformer in question to look for a place to vent (let air escape from) the transformer while the oil was drained. While Mr.

Morlan was on top of the transformer, he inadvertently came in contact with an energized lightning arrestor and suffered a serious electric shock injury.

The circumstances involved were fairly complicated, and my objective in the opening statement was to simplify and narrow the issues as much as possible. Various contract specifications and technical documents were involved in the case, but I didn't want to bore or confuse the jury by discussing too many documents during the opening statement. However, because I knew that I would refer to critical parts of Green River Steel's contract with USPCI repeatedly throughout the trial, I enlarged the relevant text of that document to poster size and used it as a demonstrative exhibit.

Opening Statement[34]

Thank you, your Honor. May it please the court and counsel and ladies and gentlemen of the jury. We'll call you the jury now because the judge went through the procedure yesterday whereby there were certain people disqualified and certain people excused.

From now on, we'll refer to you as members of the jury.

Yesterday the judge introduced various lawyers. I'm sure you'll be hearing everybody's name as the case goes on. My name is Peter Perlman, and I'm a lawyer in Lexington, Kentucky.

And yesterday there was a gentleman here named Bill Gibbes from South Carolina. Mr. Gibbes and I have had the privilege of representing Harrell Morlan, who you met yesterday, and his wife, Betty Morlan.

And you heard a lot about the case in bits and pieces yesterday, and you know something about it.

* * *

> **COMMENT:** In this case, the trial judge has conducted an extensive voir dire of the jury, discussing all the issues pertinent to the case. Additionally, because Green River Steel is a major steel production plant in Owensboro, Kentucky,

---

[34] Morlan v. Green River Steel Corp., No. 92-5952 (W.D. Ky. Mar. 6, 1992).

where the case is being tried, many of the jurors are familiar with its operation. For these reasons, I am careful not to begin the opening statement by repeating information the jurors already have.

* * *

You know what happened in Green River Steel and you heard that there was an amputation involved. Now I'm going to tell you some of the rest of the events that happened.

This case involves significant electrical injuries, and subsequently an amputation of the left arm, following an incident at the Green River Steel plant on August 22 of 1988.

This was a project where Harrell Morlan was sent to Green River Steel, here in Owensboro, by his employer. And his employer is a South Carolina environmental company. You'll hear his employer referred to as USPCI, which is United States Pollution Control, Incorporated, or PPM. I'm not real sure what that stands for, if, in fact, it stands for anything.

But you're going to learn that USPCI had contracted with Green River Steel to send some tractor trailers from South Carolina here to Owensboro to drain and transport some PCB-contaminated oil that was in some transformers.

* * *

> **COMMENT:** Although this introduction is fairly dull, I think it is necessary for setting the stage for Harrell Morlan's electrical injury. I try to cut through a lot of the technical documents and the contractual obligations of the parties and refer to the procedure in the simplest terms possible: "contracted . . . to send some tractor trailers . . . to drain and transport some PCB-contaminated oil . . . ."

* * *

You're going to learn a lot of technical things about EPA regulations and so forth, but it's really not a complicated case. The Environmental Protection Agency, within the last few years, has passed some regulations that say certain kinds of oils are toxic or potentially toxic, and you've got to get rid of them if you've got them.

So then the bids went out, and this company made a bid, and that's what the procedure was.

* * *

COMMENT: Once again, here I want to present a complicated series of events in as simple language as possible. To this end, I tell the jurors that they're going to "learn a lot of technical things . . . but it's really not a complicated case." Unless I keep the jurors' attention at the beginning of the opening statement, I may lose their interest for the remainder of the case. For this reason, in this case I eliminate many of the technical details and focus on more general issues.

* * *

Now, the whole case will surround some very narrow issues. And one of those will be whether or not some transformers were de-energized or whether they should have been de-energized.

* * *

COMMENT: Every effort should be made to reduce a case to several issues that will serve as points of reference throughout the trial.[35] There is a lot of technical language in the contracts between the parties in this case, and my objective is to eliminate the technicalities and reduce the issues to their simplest form. One of these issues is simply whether the transformers were de-energized.

* * *

And the transformers that we're talking about are the same ones that had to be drained and the oil removed. So you'll hear about Harrell Morlan, you'll hear about this event, you'll hear about his injuries, and you'll hear about what he's got to go through.

You'll learn he's had 15 surgeries of various descriptions, debridements where the tissue died. They couldn't save the arm, and he finally had to lose the arm. You're going to hear all about that.

---

[35] *See* discussion at Russ M. Herman, *supra* note 3, at 72, 74.

You're going to learn about a myoelectric arm that he has which works on electrical stimulation and that will have to be replaced from time to time as he continues.

* * *

COMMENT: I describe the injuries in a straightforward manner. The loss of an arm is a devastating injury, and the injury speaks for itself. I also introduce the jury to the fact that Mr. Morlan now needs a myoelectric arm.

In addition to providing a description of the injury, this section is intended to arouse the jurors' interest in the technology involved in replacing an amputated arm.

Before I got into this case, I thought that once an arm was replaced with a prosthetic device, the device would last forever. In working on this case, I learned that a myoelectric arm has to be replaced regularly throughout the amputee's life. Here I give the jury a preview of coming attractions about the prosthesis.

* * *

First, let me tell you about Harrell Morlan. He's 36 now; he was 33 at the time. He's married to Betty Morlan. She had one child by a previous marriage. They got married, and they've had two children.

You're going to learn about them, of his activities, their activities. You're going to learn that one of these children has a learning deficiency, and you're going to learn about some of the activities that they've been involved with, with the children and together.

You're going to learn basically that he was an over-the-road truck hauler. He has done some other work. He worked for a while in security and he worked for a while with the fire department in Columbia, South Carolina. He served in the navy.

You're going to hear about his education and his background. You're going to learn that he was active; he was athletic. He was engaged in fishing and hunting, playing with his children, and he was great at what he did.

In fact, he was recognized by his company as a driver of the year. You're going to see a plaque about that. And he took great pride in being a good over-the-road truck driver.

COMMENT: The psychological principle of identity is a major element in the trial of any case. In this section, I tell the jury that Harrell Morlan is a good person, a hard worker, a navy veteran, and a devoted family man. People appreciate someone with these qualities, and they like to think that such a person is much like themselves. It's important that you know as much as you can about your clients so you can present them in human terms.[36]

* * *

Now, this assignment that you're going to learn about and the evidence will center about will be dealing with the USPCI and Green River Steel.

Now, what you're going to learn about is that there were supposed to be two 18-wheel tanker trucks sent up here on Monday, August 22, 1988.

Their assignment was to meet a contact person, and that was the person designated by Green River Steel. That person was a man named Hollis Collier. You're going to hear him testify, and you're going to learn he was at that time the environmental engineer for Green River Steel.

And you're going to learn about some transactions involving Green River Steel and a parent company, Athlone Industries, which I believe is a New York corporation, and a contract that was entered into.

You're going to learn that on that day Harrell and another driver named Ferman Cail arrived here sometime between 8:30 and 9:00. They did what they were supposed to. They went to the plant gate; they asked for their contact person, Mr. Collier.

He met them at the gate; he told them where to drive their units to. They did that. He opened the gate, let them in at the substation. And their job at that time was to drain and transport this contaminated waste oil from two transformers.

---

[36] *See* discussion at David B. Baum, *Opening Statement*, *in* ANATOMY OF A PERSONAL INJURY LAWSUIT 205, 206 (James S. Rogers, ed., 3d ed. 1991).

COMMENT: In this section of the opening statement, I develop another theme. This theme sets up a contrast between the actions of the parties. On the one hand, the two truck drivers did everything they were supposed to do. They were there on time, they met the person they were instructed to meet, and they were ready to carry out their job assignments. This theme is developed further later in the trial through the testimony of both drivers, and on summation, I express the theme in the following manner:

> The reason we have been here throughout this trial is because Green River Steel jury-rigged these transformers and left the top energized. Harrell Morlan relied on Green River Steel's word and commitments, and he did everything he was supposed to do, and he still suffered devastating injuries. We aren't here just because he suffered these catastrophic injuries; we're here because Green River Steel *still* hasn't accepted the responsibility for its actions.

In the following portion of the opening statement, I refer the jurors to a scale model of the transformers. [See Exhibit 1.] I use the model in an attempt to simplify a fairly complicated procedure.

* * *

You're going to hear a lot of descriptions and a lot of terms. And I'm not going to try to get into all of the specifics of what everything is and what everything means right now; I'll just try and give you a general orientation.

As you can see, this is one of the transformers. This darker part here, from what I can understand, preexisted for some time; it was old equipment.

This grey part here and these bushings up here at the top were apparently added several years ago.

These units were to be drained. And there's a drain valve down here on the bottom. So you get the picture: the tanker trucks would pull up and they would hook up to that drain valve. And they would

Exhibit 1: Scale model of Green River Steel's transformers.

then suction the oil into the tanker trucks, and they would then haul it and recycle it.

So that's basically the description of the project.

* * *

COMMENT: Most people have no experience with transformers or hazardous waste disposal, and the description of the elements of this case requires special experience and handling. For this reason, I use a simple model and eliminate many of the technical details.

The jurors must realize and believe that the most important thing Green River Steel had to do before Harrell Morlan came to remove the contaminated oil was to be sure that the transformers were de-energized. Most of the previous explanations and assertions in this opening statement are there to set the stage so that the jury will "get the picture."

* * *

Now, what you're going to learn in this case is that they went to the plant gate; Mr. Collier let them in.

Before that, you're going to learn something else. You're going to learn that it's important as part of the electrical transformer, when you have truck drivers like these people come, to be sure that it has been de-energized.

And, in fact, you're going to see a letter and you're going to hear about it from USPCI, which is Mr. Morlan's employer, to Mr. Jim Bruton, who was the Electrical Director for Green River Steel, June 22, 1988, where it discusses the project and they make a quote on what they're going to do and the description of it, and how many gallons and all those details.

You're going to hear about what it's going to cost. And you see right here, it says, "Transformers are to be de-energized and made accessible to our tractor trailer vacuum unit." [See Exhibit 2.]

* * *

COMMENT: Although there are many contractual documents involved in the transaction between USPCI and

USPCI, INC.

June 22, 1988

Mr. Jim Bruton
Green River Steel
4701 US 60 East
Owensboro, KY 42303

Re: Detoxification of PCB-Contaminated Oil

Dear Mr. Bruton:

USPCI/PPM, Inc. is pleased to provide Green River Steel with the following quote:

For the off-site chemical detoxification of 9,400 gallons of PCB-contaminated oil, generated from the two 4,235 gallon units, including tap changers containing 465 gallons each at the steel mill in Owensboro:

Oils will be hauled off in bulk vacuum units and brought to a designated annex for detoxification.

Transformers are to be de-energized, and made accessible to our tractor trailer vacuum unit.

Price per gallon to be $0.78.

Price per mile to be $3.35 at 400 miles.

Demurrage to be billed at $65.00 per hour, if loading takes longer than two hours. Two vehicles will be required, and can be scheduled as Green River Steel directs.

Any price per gallon, based on 9,400 gallons, to be ±$1.07 per gallon, delivered price.

(Continued)

Exhibit 2: Reproduction of letter from USPCI to Green River Steel.

Exhibit 2, continued.

> Certificate of Decontamination will be returned to green River Steel within 14 days receipt of bulk shipments.
>
> If I can provide any additional information, or be of any assistance to you, please feel free to contact me at (404) 934-0902.
>
> Sincerely,
>
> Kent Woodward, Jr.
> Senior Sales Representative
>
> KW/dcg

Green River Street, I chose to limit the references to these documents in the opening statement. Documents of this sort are not likely to capture the imagination or interest of the jury, and it's best to avoid referring to numerous documents in opening statements. However, this document—a letter from USPCI to Green River—is critical, and its contents become a recurring theme in the case. The letter sets forth various terms and specifically states the most important element of the transaction:

> Transformers are to be de-energized and made accessible to our tractor trailer vacuum unit.

* * *

There's no question about this letter, and you're going to hear a lot about it. It's signed by Kent Woodward, who was the sales representative for USPCI. But there's no question, and I don't believe there's going to be any question but that this letter was a part of the transaction, that it was to be de-energized before they got there and that there wasn't going to be any power, so that when they drained the transformer, they could do it safely and get on and get out. It's a routine project, and you're going to hear that this is a routine provision when they do these things.

What had happened was that this thing had been out of service for some time. And sometime shortly before June of 1988, they apparently decided to take the transformers off of power. But they didn't take the top portions off of electrical power.

You're going to hear some explanations about why they did that, and you're going to be able to listen to that testimony.

But what you're going to learn about is that on August 22, 1988, there was a serious injury, and a serious catastrophe involving several people was just barely avoided.

* * *

> **COMMENT:** Once again, I assert that the failure to de-energize the transformer is the event that caused catastrophic consequences. Not only did Mr. Morlan suffer an injury, Green River Steel's own environmental director barely escaped injury.

* * *

You're going to learn a lot. First, you're going to learn about the letter and the terms. And then you're going to hear from Mr. Woodward, who signed this letter. And Mr. Woodward's going to say that some time after that bid was accepted and sometime after this project was undertaken, he came to Owensboro himself, the senior sales representative for USPCI.

He met with the people here; he met with Mr. Collier, the environmental engineer. And he met with Mr. Bruton, the electrical person. And he looked over the project. And the one thing that he's going to say that was the key to the meeting was that he insisted, and they assured him, that all the power would be shut off. The units were to be de-energized.

There's not any qualification about that. It's not going to be, "Well, parts of them should be and parts of them shouldn't be . . . ." You're going to hear that since truck drivers are merely hauling stuff away, they're not supposed to know what parts are de-energized and what parts are not.

The units were to be de-energized. And the "unit" would be the entire unit, from here to the top. And there's another one just like it.

COMMENT: The defense in this case was that each transformer was a two-part unit: the lower part had been de-energized, but the top part containing the lightning arrestors had not been de-energized. The reason given was that the wiring to the factory needed to be maintained.

In reality, the lightning arrestor setup was devised because Green River Steel's management had decided that it would be cheaper to maintain electrical power by leaving the top portion of the transformer energized than to rewire.

Unfortunately, management did't tell even its own environmental director that a portion of the transformer was still energized. As a result, he didn't know this vital fact, and therefore he was not in a position to advise Mr. Morlan.

* * *

So they had two trucks and they were going to drain and transport the oil from the two units.

So what you're going to find out is, before this day, Green River Steel didn't check the transformers to be sure they were de-energized. They didn't inspect the transformers to be sure that this project could be done safely.

They did not establish any procedures—any—to vent and drain these transformers. And you're going to learn that's important because to be able to drain something like this, you've got to have a vent in place. And they had no procedure.

They didn't provide any knowledgeable personnel, either the contact person or anybody else, that knew how to vent and drain this, or that knew how to de-energize it, as it turned out.

* * *

COMMENT: The failure of Green River personnel to perform even basic procedures is a recurring theme. Because this case is fairly technical, with many specialized terms and procedures involved, my emphasizing the corporate personnel's failure to perform even the most basic safeguards is an effective way to simplify the issues involved.

After this theme is introduced in the opening statement, it is reaffirmed throughout the trial.[37]

* * *

And when they left the top part energized, they did that in order to bypass these transformers so that they could keep some kind of limited function. And you're going to hear various descriptions of what that was—whether they were surge arrestors or lightning arrestors.

So we come now to Monday, August 22, sometime between 8:30 and 9:00. The two tractor trailer units arrive, go to the guard gate. Mr. Collier is the contact person. Mr. Collier is called; he escorts them to the substation, and he opens the gate with a key. Two times after they get to the substation, Harrell Morlan says, "Now, I want to be sure these things are de-energized."

There's not going to be any dispute about it. Harrell Morlan's going to tell you that; Ferman Cail, the other driver, is going to tell you that; and Mr. Collier himself is going to tell you, "Yeah, they asked were they de-energized."

And both times he said, "Yes, they are." And Mr. Collier believed they were.

* * *

COMMENT: Now I am describing the actual activities on August 22, the fateful day when Harrell Morlan suffered his devastating injury. By now the jury realizes how important it was to de-energize the transformers.

* * *

And they walked around. And anybody who's been around electrical equipment knows you can tell whether something is energized either by vibration or by the sound of it. And Harrell felt it and it wasn't vibrating. And you couldn't hear it.

So he had another positive signal that the thing was off; there wasn't any power.

---

[37] *Id.* at 208.

COMMENT: An effective opening statement should also anticipate the defenses that will be raised. One of the defenses in this case is that Harrell Morlan should not have simply relied on Green River's personnel but should have done more to be sure that the transformers were not energized. Here I anticipate and counteract that defense by telling the jury that Mr. Morlan did do more. He felt the transformer, and he couldn't feel vibrations or hear any electrical noises.

* * *

So Harrell said, "Mr. Collier, are these things vented? Are they ready to go?"

Mr. Collier said, "They're ready to go, but I don't know about this venting."

So Hollis Collier didn't know about how to vent it, and there wasn't anybody there who did. And you're going to hear that that was Green River Steel's responsibility.

But Mr. Collier requested a ladder. He radioed, apparently, Mr. Bruton, the electrical person. Mr. Bruton sent a ladder.

And Harrell said, "I don't know where you could vent it, but sometimes on these things you might be able to go on top and find a place."

Thinking everything was safe and everything was shut off, Mr. Collier climbed the ladder.

* * *

COMMENT: The model gives the case a new dimension. An oral description of an electrical transformer is pretty unexciting. For this reason we obtain a scale model and try to make it look as lifelike as possible, even making several to-scale figures, little people with moveable arms and legs. The model is authenticated for use in trial in the same way that photographs and other visual evidence are authenticated. We establish that it is a scale model and that it fairly and accurately depicts the transformer and surrounding structures.

Now, I believe the ladder was right there where it is now. And this model here is three quarters of an inch to one foot. So that gives you a scale.

So Mr. Collier climbed the ladder; he got up here on this side of it; he's looking around.

He says, "I don't see anything up here." So he says, "Why don't you come up here and help me?"

So Harrell Morlan climbs up this ladder. He gets up here and they're up there together. Both of them thinking, this is safe, everything's been shut off.

The letter said so; Mr. Woodward was assured of that; Harrell Morlan was assured of that; Mr. Collier was assured of that.

* * *

COMMENT: Once again, I repeat the liability theme. Now that the jury has seen the model and has learned the importance of de-energizing the transformer, I simplify the language even further. Instead of talking about de-energizing, I now talk about everything being shut off.

* * *

So Harrell is up there, and he crawls on his hands and knees through this little trough here between these two areas, looking for a place to vent. And there are some places.

You're going to learn that there is a place to vent up there.

So he gets up here and he turns around and he stands up and either he says, "We may try this," or he's thinking that there is a place.

Before he knows it, he's hit with a massive zap, knocked backwards, still on the edge over here; he's been hit with electricity.

You're going to hear it described in various ways, like a flash and a sudden zap. Now, Mr. Cail will tell you that it sounded like one of those bug zappers that you have in the summertime.

And he's down and he's got blood. Ultimately his shirt's on fire. You're going to learn all about this.

It was a tragic, horrendous situation.

* * *

COMMENT: At what point should damages be discussed

during the opening statement? In a case of this sort, I discuss the liability first and then develop the damages. I briefly mention the nature of the injury at the beginning of the opening statement; the jurors already know from voir dire that there has been a serious electrical injury with a resulting amputation of the arm. Certainly I might choose to develop the damages to a greater extent at an earlier point during the opening statement, but in this case I choose instead to develop the circumstances that lead up to the injury and then proceed to discuss the damages involved.

* * *

Now while he's still laying up here, Mr. Bruton, the electrical engineer, goes to a little house somewhere and shuts off the circuit breaker.

But while that's being done, you've still got three people up here. Mr. Collier's still down here; Mr. Cail is over here attending to his friend and his buddy. All three of them are still exposed to this energized transformer up here.

I don't know that anybody will know whether Harrell inadvertently touched something or whether he inadvertently touched a wire.

But whatever he did up there, he did with the full assurance that the transformer was de-energized.

You're also going to hear that the sound was consistent with an arcing sound. And you don't have to touch anything when it's energized for it to arc. Whether you touch it or not, it touches you. Electricity can be just as deadly whether you touch it or not.

* * *

COMMENT: In this section, I discuss with the jury the dangerous aspects of electricity. This is not a technical explanation, but a simple overview. Later in the trial, the expert testimony will show that a person can be hurt even without touching a wire.

* * *

So there's not going to be any question that he got burned. You're going to see the pictures and where the electricity touched him on the stomach and on the hand, and then he had skin grafts on his back and on the back of his leg. And you're going to see the effects of the electricity.

Now, whether or not he actually touched something—he's going to say he doesn't think he did—he sure didn't intend to. And there's not going to be any definite testimony on that one way or the other, because you can be just as badly hurt whether you touch it or not because of the arcing principle.

The case is about basic safety. Green River Steel and the Athlone Industries who contracted this project failed to do a lot. They failed to provide a safe work environment. They failed to take any safety precautions. They failed to de-energize a silent assassin in the form of this electrical transformer.

But worst of all, the evidence in this case will be that they represented not once, but several times, that they had done it.

* * *

COMMENT: Once again I go back to the overall theme of the case, which is "basic safety." I introduce the theme in the beginning of the opening statement, then go into some detail on the specific unsafe acts, and here give the theme again.

Now that I've explained to the jury a little bit about the way electricity works, I use the words "a silent assassin." I also carry over this language and use it during the closing argument.

* * *

The damages you might expect in a case like this are catastrophic. Harrell Morlan has had some 15 surgeries, some lasting four to eight hours, where the tissue had died and they had to go through all kinds of procedures, debridements, and skin grafting.

And you're going to hear all about that, and it was painful. And the hospital and medical expenses alone are about $197,000. He was in the hospital for six weeks right off the bat, from the time this thing happened for six more weeks.

He's had a prosthesis. He's had a myoelectric arm that you're going to see, and it works through electrical stimulation. And it only had a life expectancy of so many years. So a specialist in that area is going to testify that that's got to be replaced. And that's expensive.

* * *

COMMENT: The last several years have seen much improvement in prosthetics technology. In the past, a prosthetic device generally consisted of a simple imitation of the amputated extremity. Such a device was either nonfunctional or severely limited in function, and it served primarily as a cosmetic substitute.

Present-day technology provides a myoelectric prosthesis that performs many of the functions of the human arm. The prosthesis is controlled through electrodes that receive and interpret impulses from the remaining muscles of the upper arm. While the new prosthesis is a great improvement over previous devices, it is expensive and has to be replaced frequently, and testimony to that effect should be developed at length in an amputation case. In this case this testimony is provided by Edward Gormanson, a certified prosthetist. Mr. Gormanson's video deposition was presented at the trial, and he describes the myoelectric arm:

> The myoelectric [arm] is a system that is controlled through the brain. We attach electrodes to the muscles of his forearm by mounting these within the socket. And the skin touches these electrodes.
>
> Once he makes a muscle contraction the electric hand responds to the muscle contraction. It either closes with one muscle contraction or opens with an antagonistic muscle contraction or opposite muscle contraction. (Deposition p. 10.)

In addition, Mr. Gormanson explains the advantages of the myoelectric arm over the conventional prosthetic arm, which consists of a cosmetic limb that is attached to the amputee with a shoulder harness and that has a specialized hook instead of a hand:

> [The myoelectric arm is] more cosmetic, seeing as how it has a more realistic hand than a hook. It also

> provides more function for the amputee. It holds and stabilizes things more than a hook would and provides the holding ability so things will not slip out of the hand, whereas a hook is very limited in function and in the area you can work it.
>
> With this harness on and strapped on, [when] you put the arm behind your body, the harness is loose and you can't open the hook. With the electric hand, anyplace you can put your hand and separate those muscle signals above your head, below your back, down by your feet, anyplace you put the hand the hand will work. (Deposition pp. 12–13.)

* * *

He missed some 44 weeks from his work. You're not going to hear that this man was sitting at home and not doing anything—because he did go back to work. He's not back as a truck driver, but his employer took him back and put him into a job as a dispatcher. So now he's inside. And he's doing that work; he's working regularly.

Despite the fact that he's working, you're going to hear that he's got a diminished earning capacity. And a vocational expert named Gary Shaw will tell you what that is. Sure, he may be able to work now in a certain job with certain conditions. But in a competitive environment with the injuries that he's got, he's severely limited. And that's a diminished earning capacity and you're going to hear about that.

* * *

COMMENT: By the date of the trial, Harrell Morlan has been rehired by his former employer. However, he has been given an indoor position as a dispatcher, not his former job as a truck driver. According to the medical testimony we will hear later in the case, Mr. Morlan has suffered a 49-percent impairment to his entire body because of the loss of his left arm. The vocational expert testifies that a man with this kind of injury and the other injuries suffered by Mr. Morlan is severely restricted on the competitive labor market. In addition, he testifies that most manual labor jobs will not be available for someone with these injuries.

And Betty Morlan—in a case like this under the law, she has a separate case. It's called loss of consortium. Because by reason of the injuries to her husband, her life has been changed. You're going to hear about that—the things that he would do and the things that they would do and the difference in their lives. And she's entitled to fair and reasonable compensation.

This will basically be the evidence that we will present. At the conclusion of the case, we are going to ask you to do only one thing: to be fair and to be reasonable. And under the law that's all that the jury can do and that's all we're going to ask you to do.

But I believe that when the case is over, that "fair" and "reasonable" will demand a substantial verdict because these are substantial and catastrophic injuries and this was a horrendous event that should not have happened.

Thank you.

* * *

COMMENT: You always want to end the opening statement on a high note. In this case, I use strong language. I go on to use much of the language I use here—"substantial damages," "catastrophic injuries," and "horrendous event"—throughout the trial and on summation.

About the Author

Peter Perlman, a successful trial lawyer with a practice in Lexington, Kentucky, is active in academia and writing. He is a professor at the University of Kentucky College of Law, and he serves on both the Advisory Board of the *American Journal of Trial Advocacy* and the Board of Editors of the *Trial Diplomacy Journal*. His writings have been published in books, law journals, and CLE materials.

Perlman received his undergraduate degree and his law degree from the University of Kentucky. He is active in professional organizations and has served as president of both ATLA and the Kentucky Academy of Trial Lawyers. He is currently a trustee of the Roscoe Pound Foundation and of the Civil Justice Foundation, a member of the Inner Circle of Advocates, and a fellow of the American Bar Association.